JOYFUL IN MY HOUSE OF PRAYER

JOYFUL IN MY HOUSE OF PRAYER

PRAYER

GEORGE MCAULIFFE'S TESTIMONY

BRENDAN MCCAULEY

McCauley Books

India - One Act of Kindness
Better Than Weapons of War
A Man of Ethiopia
Staying Alive!
Joyful In My House Of Prayer
The Grapes Are Worth It!
All God's Bible Dreams
Look At The Birds

And they overcame Satan
by the blood of the Lamb and
by the word of their testimony, and
they did not love their lives to the
death.

Revelation 12:11

In Irish society, the Seanchai were the storytellers that took on that age-old tradition of the "Filí" – poets and historians who captured history, genealogies, customs and magic in story and verse.

CONTENTS

A NEW PENTECOST

THIS IS the story of how Jesus Christ revealed himself to George and Sheila McAuliffe from Milltown, Co. Kerry and how He filled them with His Holy Spirit and showed them signs and wonders they never thought possible.

My wife Angela and I from Northern Ireland, and George and Sheila from the Republic of Ireland were fairly typical Catholics going about our daily business when God came into our lives during a move of His Holy Spirit in Ireland in the 1970s.

God did the choosing and we responded. We gave ourselves to Jesus and were baptised in His Holy Spirit, spoke in tongues and prophesied and received various gifts and graces of the Holy Spirit.

We met George and Sheila in 1985. They were around ten years older than us. We loved their warm welcome and gentle wisdom and we grew to value their friendship.

George and Sheila remained within the Catholic Church and held a Thursday night weekly prayer meeting in their own home for over forty years. Angela and I on the other hand went on a long prophetic journey that took us through various denominations and into many nations.

Sheila died suddenly in her early sixties and George died over a dozen years later. George missed Sheila every single day.

A couple of years before George's death I was ministering around Ireland with my Canadian friend Lionel Batke. We were staying in Abbeyfeale, Co. Limerick, with John and Angela Browne. Early on the Friday morning I had a dream in which I was told to go urgently and interview George and write a book about his testimony of Jesus. God said if I'd do this for Him then He'd make the time up to me.

A couple of years earlier George had asked me to write a book about his experiences with Jesus. On another occasion George said he'd only have one regret in life and that would be if he went to his grave without his experiences with Jesus being told.

I arranged Lionel would take the remaining meetings and I went and spent the weekend with George. The following story comes from that encounter. I've written the book in the first person because that's how it came to me as I sat listening to George.

In 1959 Pope John XIII at the 'sudden inspiration' of the Holy Spirit called for the first ecumenical council for the Roman Catholic Church. Part of that council's purpose was to foster Christian unity and an other part was the Pope's prayer that the council might be a 'New Pentecost' for the Catholic Church.

George likened the Pope's prayer to an experience he had as a young boy on the family farm in Brosna.

George said, My father kept an untamed donkey. Day after day my sister and I pestered him to let us to ride this headstrong animal.

Finally, one warm summer's day Dad hauled the donkey into the hay shed and put my sister on its back. The donkey bolted and my sister screamed. She had daily petitioned Dad for months but her donkey ride lasted only a few seconds.

I insisted on my turn. Once more Neddy was dragged into the hay shed and this time Dad placed me on his back and gave me the reins.

Once again he bolted but I had a plan. I grabbed his mane with my right hand, clutched his tail with my left hand and held on for dear life.

Off we went! Twice around the house, once down the field and back up again we galloped. I was fully determined but so was Neddy.

In the end I found myself lying in a dry ditch with a sore body and a bruised ego.

I sometimes think our encounter with Dad's donkey was a lot like Pope John XXIII asking for a New Pentecost in the Catholic Church.

GRIEF SURELY LEADING ME

AFTER MASS ON SAINT PATRICK'S Day, 1973, Sheila and I and our three children, Muireann, David and Emer drove to see my parents on their farm in Brosna. My father wasn't well. On the way we stopped to visit my brother Willie who was recovering from a hernia operation in the Bon's Hospital in Tralee.

In the backseat, Muireann aged four and David aged three were talking.

Muireann said, Yes David, Daddy is my daddy.

David said, No he's not. He's my daddy.

The debate continued then David offered a compromise. He said, Muireann, Let him be my daddy. You can have the dog.

I first met my wife Sheila nine years earlier in 1964. That year I'd finished a Higher Diploma in Education and had volunteered to go teaching with the Kiltegan

Fathers in Minna in west central Nigeria. In September of that year this option quickly disappeared when militant Muslims overran Minna College.

Unusually, I was offered a job teaching in a Girl's Convent School. Later I moved to a boy's school, The Presentation Secondary School in Milltown, Co Kerry and found lodgings above a newsagent's shop.

One Sunday after Mass I was sitting in the parlour reading *The Independent* when a beautiful young lady walked into the room with a large smile and a twinkle in her eye.

She offered her hand and said, Mr McAuliffe I believe!

I said, George McAuliffe at your service.

Now we were happily married in a car full of life and laughter. We soon arrived into the hospital car park. Sheila remained with the children while I made a quick call on my brother.

When I returned Sheila looked puzzled.

I said, What happened?

Sheila said David had pointed to the large statue in the Hospital car park and asked, Mammy, who's that in the corner.

Sheila said, That's a statue of St. Joseph, son.

David said, Mammy, St. Joseph will take me up to heaven.

Sheila thought this was a strange response from our little son. She took a notebook from her handbag and wrote and dated this remark. That little blue notebook remained in the car for years.

On the farm David sang songs and my mother nursed little Emer. It was a warm happy day. I remember my father's laughter as we chatted over lunch. I then stayed behind to look after Dad for a couple of days.

When I returned home to Milltown, David was leafing through an old catalogue. Shortly after he went to bed I heard a noise from his room. I was taking Lemsip for a cold I couldn't quite shake off. When I entered David's room he spied the cup and said, Thanks Da. He thought the hot drink was for him.

Though normally I wouldn't allow him up after he'd gone to bed I said, David would you like to come downstairs?

He jumped at the chance. Downstairs he again grabbed the catalogue and sat on my lap. He opened the pages and pointed. He said things like, Dan Daddy I'm going to buy you this. Dan Daddy I'm going to buy you that.

He promised me the sun, the moon and the stars. When I carried him back to bed he started singing,

Daddy McAuliffe is a great good boy!

Daddy McAuliffe is a great good boy!

He kept singing the same words over and over again. I didn't know it at the time but David was delirious from the effects of a cancerous tumour in his kidney.

This was Monday 19th March 1973 – St Joseph's feast day.

Next day when I came home for lunch David was lying on the sofa looking very pale. He kept saying, Oh blast, Mammy, my back! Oh blast, Mammy, my back!

We took him to hospital where he was kept in for tests.

On Friday I was called to speak to a visiting consultant. While I was waiting for the appointment an old nun shuffled over and sat down.

She said, God still heals and miracles can happen.

I thought, What on earth is she talking about?

The more she talked the more annoyed I became. I felt rescued when my name was called.

I sat across from the consultant. I asked, Have you met this condition in children before?

He said, Yes I have.

I said, And how are the children doing now?

He hemmed and hawed and looked at his pen.

I knew they were all dead.

My sister Eilish, a nurse in Cork, arrived at this point. The consultant suggested we take David to Dublin's Crumlin Hospital.

Eilish said, Why not take him to St Finnbar's in Cork?

He said, St Finbarr's will do fine.

It seemed it didn't matter where we took him. Now I understood what the old nun was talking about. Someone had told her David was going to die.

That evening Sheila and I drove David to St Finnbar's. We had a puncture on the way. While I was changing the wheel David poked his head out of the passenger window and sang,

Daddy's shirt peeping out.

Daddy's shirt peeping out.

He thought it was a game. We sang more songs. As we neared the city, Sheila started singing, *Nearer my God to me*, the Catholic version from St Basil's Hymnal:

Nearer, my God, to Thee, nearer to Thee!
E'en though it be a cross that raiseth me,
Still all my song shall be, nearer, my God,
    to Thee.
Nearer, my God, to Thee, nearer to Thee!
Deep in thy Sacred Heart let me abide.
Thou that has bled for me, sorrowed and
    died.
Sweet shall me weeping be, grief surely
    leading me,
Nearer, my God, to Thee, nearer to Thee!

The words *grief surely leading me* kept running through my mind. I thought to myself, George you thought education might lead you. Gaelic sport might lead you. Politics might lead you. Facts might lead you. Philosophy might lead you. Knowledge might lead you. Theology might lead you. Hard work might lead you. But you never thought grief would ever lead you.

This was a completely new concept. Now something unknown to me was happening. Something I'd no words for. Something bigger and independent of me. Was I was being presented with an opportunity that didn't look like an opportunity?

PADRE PIO CAME TO SEE ME

SHORTLY AFTER DAVID'S diagnosis Sheila and I went to my home church of St Moling & St Carthage in Brosna and lit a candle. We were the only ones in the building.

I said, Sheila I believe the way we're meant to face this situation is to view it as if we were looking back at it from thirty years in the future. So that in thirty years time we can look back on 1973 and say, We're glad we responded in the way we did.

I felt it was as if we were being given the gift of hindsight prior to the challenge. Afterwards we'd often say there wasn't one single thing we'd have done differently in 1973. This idea of thirty years into the future became a framework from which we operated. It gave us perspective and enabled us not to be overwhelmed by our grief.

We've often said 1973 was the best year of our lives

for it was David's sickness and death that started us on a path that eventually led us to Jesus Christ as our Lord and Saviour. And from the scriptures we also gained the joy of knowing we'd see David again in heaven.

Prior to David's death I was really only a cultural Catholic. Often I'd find myself at Mass wondering what it was all about. I suppose I gave mental assent to all of the doctrines of the Catholic Church. If they taught transubstantiation then I believed in transubstantiation. Who was I not to believe?

The same went for The Immaculate Conception, Papal Infallibility and a host of other beliefs. Who was I not to believe? Was I a learned theologian?

If there'd been a new edict from the Second Vatican Council saying there were now four persons in God then I'd probably have gone along with that too.

Those were the days when doctors, teachers and priests had great power and authority. The doctor wrote you a prescription in a script you couldn't read and you took it without question. The priest gave you penance for sins and you didn't disagree.

David was in an isolation ward. We weren't supposed to visit but I went in anyway. He was thrilled to see me. His eyes were full of joy. There were twelve beds in the ward. David was in the corner one, lying without a toy or a picture book. I sat down and held his hand.

He said, Daddy what will I be doing in heaven?

His little brown eyes were so earnest.

I said, David you'll be praying for Mammy and Daddy in heaven.

He said, Ah no Daddy. I'm too small to pray.

I said, You'll be looking after Mammy and Daddy so.

He said, I will.

I had a regular routine during the summer school holidays. I'd stay in Cork with my sister Marie to be near the hospital. I'd sleep from 9.30pm to 4.30am and I'd be at David's bedside before 5am. He'd be awake with a big smile.

His first words always were, Daddy sing a flew songs. He couldn't say few. I'd always start with *Brosna Town*:

> My dear old home in the Kerry Hills, my
> thoughts are still with thee
> Although I'm in a foreign land across the
> deep blue sea
> I long to stand outside your door and
> watch the sun go down
> And hear the church bells tolling o'er my
> native Brosna town
> By the old wood road I long to stroll with
> its hedge's tall and green
> By Hannon's gate, I would debate with
> some lovely fair colleen

Or take a walk to Guine's bridge on a
   Sunday afternoon
Where oft I danced a polka set to a lively
   fiddlers tune

Just David and me singing songs and holding hands. At 5:20am I'd say, David I have to go now but I'll be back later. His trusting eyes knew I'd keep my word.

At 5:30am I'd attend mass in the nearby Catholic church. Afterwards I'd walk to another Catholic church and so on. From 5.30am to 9.30am each morning I'd be at Mass in various churches. Then I'd spend more time with David. Sheila would come later.

One morning David said, Daddy, Padre Pio came to see me last night.

I didn't know how to respond. I said, Did he so?

When David took sick, some people gave us copies of prayers to say. One was a prayer to Padre Pio. I wondered if David had seen this prayer.

But David was adamant. He said it was Padre Pio himself who came to see him.

Around this time Sheila and I became friendly with Donal Enright a local Padre Pio devotee. One day Donal visited with one of Padre Pio's mitts and prayed for David. Afterwards he said, George, if David is cured you might do a pilgrimage to San Giovanni.

To my surprise I said, Sure I'm going to San Giovanni anyway.

Never in my life had I ever intended to go to San Giovanni and here I was saying, I'm going anyway.

I said, I'm not into doing deals with God. If God heals David, well and good but I'm going to bring him to San Giovanni anyway. Let God do what he will do. I will do what I will do.

I told Sheila my intentions and although we were tight for money she said, No problem at all, Seoirse. We'll go and take David.

Sheila often affectionately called me Seoirse, the Irish for George.

We decided on October. On our flight to Lourdes we sat behind Joe Lynch and his wife. Joe was president of the Irish Handball Association. Joe didn't know me but I knew him for I was playing a lot of handball in North Kerry at the time. Sheila and Joe's wife started talking.

Joe's wife said, We're not stopping off at Lourdes at all. We're going on to Rome to meet a Catholic mystic who has the stigmata.

As soon as she mentioned the mystic I instantly knew I would also meet this man. I said nothing to Sheila at this point. I didn't know how to explain to her my sudden knowledge that I'd meet this Catholic mystic.

After a couple of days in Lourdes we went on to Rome. There we were met by our two friends Christie McElwee from Northern Ireland and Richard Sharma from the West Indies. They were studying for the Rosminian priesthood.

We were chatting over coffee in the Hotel Adrianna when I told Christie and Richard that I'd like to meet this certain Catholic mystic. Sheila looked strangely at me. They said they hadn't heard of this mystic but they would make inquiries.

Next day David and I headed off to the tomb of Padre Pio in San Giovanni Rotondo. Sheila wasn't interested. She went off shopping with some ladies.

It was a long journey by train, nearly 400 kilometres. We boarded a carriage with five soldiers. One of our friends spoke to the soldiers in Italian and explained we needed to get off at Barri station in order to take a bus to San Giovanni.

When the soldiers alighted at their stop they explained to the remaining passengers to look after us and to make sure we got off at the right place. One of the soldiers was an artist. He drew sketches of lakes and boats and birds for David. He also let David draw bits and pieces. We kept these pictures for ages afterwards.

From Barri we travelled the last 50 kilometres to San Giovanni along a mountainous road in an old hot rickety bus.

San Giovanni Rotondo was a beautiful piazza. David and I were the only people there. We walked around sightseeing and went to Padre Pio's tomb in the middle of the church. For some reason I wanted to place David on top of the tomb but there were railings preventing me.

Suddenly there was a rattle of keys and two women scurrying towards us with mop buckets. They opened the gate to the tomb and before they knew it David and I were also inside the railing. The women were flustered but when I gestured my desire they nodded their heads. One of them took David and set him on top of Padre Pio's tomb.

As we were leaving the church David turned to me and said, Daddy I'm not going to die at all. It's you who's going to die.

I said, David I don't think that arrangement would solve our problems either.

That was the end of that conversation but I often wondered about it.

I carried David on my back around the piazza. At a spot near the middle I was struck by the sweet smell of perfume. I couldn't see where it was coming from. I walked over to a flower bed about forty yards away. Once I moved away from the sweet spot the smell of perfume disappeared. It definitely wasn't coming from the flowers.

I walked back to the sweet spot and the beautiful smell was still there. I moved in the opposite direction to see if the fragrance was coming from that direction and as I moved away from the sweet spot, again the beautiful scent disappeared. In the end I eliminated every other part of the piazza except the middle bit where the fragrance was heady and strong.

I was standing pondering this phenomenon when a young Capuchin monk came walking towards me. I recognised him. It was Padre Alessio who'd been Padre Pio's minder and servant. I'd seen him on *The Late Late Show with Gay Byrne* on Irish Television a couple of years previously. We started chatting.

Padre Alessio was warm and hospitable. He showed us around. We visited Padre Pio's bedroom and the oratory where Padre Pio received the stigmata. David and I spent all afternoon with Padre Alessio. There was only David, the cleaning ladies, the perfume, Padre Alessio and myself in this special place on this special day.

There were no empty seats on the train back to Rome. I sat on the floor with David on my knee. He was bothered with the heat. I ordered Orange juice. David became annoyed. He pushed the litre of juice into my face, over my glasses and down my shirt.

I felt so sorry for him. This was so unlike David. A little tender child tired and troubled, turning on the one who truly loved him. I wasn't angry. In fact the more annoyed he became the more I loved him and cared for him. As the train rattled along he soon fell asleep in my arms.

As I listened to his breathing I realised just how much I was often like David in that little incident. So often I'd rejected God and His offer of love. So often I'd thrown good things back into His face. But like me with David, God loved me all the more.

I had travelled to San Giovanni Rotunda hoping to find some answer and although we had a wonderful time, I felt I still hadn't found what I was looking for. But as I sat on that crowded train I realised no matter how much I'd kick against God and blame him for this thing and that thing He would still love me. I might reject God but God would never reject me.

In my confusion I might fuss and fume but He would never stop loving me. He really was my Father in Heaven. I felt God had spoken to me in my difficulties. I'd found this little treasure in a darkened corner on the dusty floor of a packed Italian train. I wasn't angry with David. My heart broke for his plight. I would happily have given my life for his life.

Back in Rome our friends had located the mystic at a place twelve miles away. They and Sheila were amused at my desire to meet this mystic but they were happy enough to humour me. The mystic's place was a massive building site of rubble and sand and cement. There was a queue outside an old Nissan hut that doubled up as an oratory and chapel.

Sheila and Christie and Richard went sightseeing and David and I joined the queue for a ruddy-faced man who was distributing holy pictures. There were about twenty people ahead of us. When we neared the front of the queue the man with the pictures looked up and stared at David with blue piercing eyes. Turned out this was the mystic. We received our holy picture and stepped outside into the sunlight.

We hung around waiting for Sheila and our friends who soon came back smiling and laughing. We stood chatting while David played in a pile of sand. A door behind David opened and the mystic came out and turned left. David was standing nearby. The mystic stopped and very slowly and carefully placed his stigmatic hands upon David's head and prayed.

Sheila and I and our friends all watched this but I saw something completely different from them. If there was a recording made of this incident you would have heard me repeating the phrase, *Isn't that extraordinary. Isn't that extraordinary?*

I was gobsmacked. All around the mystic was a huge ball of silver light accompanied by a sweet smelling perfume and a humming noise. This sound lasted the whole time he prayed with David. He them turned and still glowing with silver light walked to another door about forty yards away. All during this I kept saying, *Isn't that extraordinary?*

I turned to Sheila and our friends. I said, Wasn't that light and perfume and buzzing sound amazing?

Sheila said, What light and perfume and buzzing sound?

They heard no sound, smelt no perfume and saw no

light. They only saw the mystic praying for David. I thought about this. There were eight eyes looking in the same direction. Six saw nothing unusual and two saw silver light. I must have had a vision.

David was in good humour on the flight home but was visibly growing weaker by the day. Soon after we arrived home he was called in for chemotherapy.

SOMETHING BEAUTIFUL
FOR GOD

ON HOLY SATURDAY Midnight Mass in 1973, one of the scripture readings was from Genesis 22 about God asking Abraham for the life of his beloved son Isaac.

The Mass leaflet said people who are suffering would probably benefit most from this reading. This was a strange statement but it resonated with Sheila and me and during that Mass we chose to respond like Abraham and willingly allow God to take the life of our beloved son David if that's what He wanted.

We said, Yes, to God! In Abraham's case he had to do the killing but in our case cancer was taking David's life and we had little choice in the matter. Afterwards we never reneged on this *Yes* or ever resisted the unfolding events.

During that Mass I remembered the famous Mother Teresa phrase, *Something beautiful for God.* I kept hearing those words throughout the Mass and in the end I believed something beautiful could come out of our pain and sorrow and the loss of David.

Afterwards we were sometimes tempted to revert back into traditional religion and just become cultural Catholics again. Often this appeared an easier route. No pressure. Let someone else do the thinking. Not having to be led by the Holy Spirit. Not having to walk by faith. But when we'd be tempted to doubt we would think back to that Holy Saturday Night and that first big *Yes* to God.

Intuitively we knew our first *Yes* contained within it thousands of other *Yeses* but we also knew God would strengthen us for our journey. There was great comfort in that Sheila and I were in unity about this choice. Our agreement made it bearable.

It seemed as if two roads diverged in that Holy Saturday Midnight Mass and we took the one less travelled. We decided to walk in the ancient pathway where we'd find rest for our souls. We chose to let God be God. We opted to believe all things would work together for the good of those who loved the Lord. And that made all the difference.

Years later a friend called Pat Cahill came to one of our meetings. Pat would occasionally go into ecstasy during worship. He did so that night and during his ecstasy he rapidly flicked through his Bible page after page with his eyes closed. He suddenly stopped with his finger on Romans 4.

He then opened his eyes and read the chapter, which was all about Abraham believing God and being justified by faith. He looked at me and said, George I believe God is comparing you to Abraham in this passage. Abraham believed God and it was credited to him as righteousness. I think God is saying the same thing to you.

The call and the dilemma of Abraham and Sarah have been important to Sheila and me since David's death. The loss of a beloved son was very important to them and us. They had the same feelings and misgivings as we had. We were all part of planet Earth. We slept in the same way. We hoped in the same way. We were just ordinary people God touched and called for God's purposes.

Fathers have to do hard things sometimes. The final time David was in hospital I made an unscheduled visit. The large ward was deathly quiet. I was only allowed in for a few minutes. I took David in my arms and held him close. I wanted to hold him forever but all too soon I was asked to leave. As I did so, for the only time during any of his hospital stays, David cried his heart out.

I tucked him into bed and said, Son I'm so sorry but I really have to go now.

As I walked down the corridor I could still hear him crying and calling, *Daddy come back, Daddy come back!*

My heart was tearing in two.

Yet alongside David's pleas I could also hear words within my spirit from Galatians,

> I have been crucified with Christ and I no
> longer live, but Christ lives in me. The
> life I now live in the body, I live by
> faith in the Son of God, who loved me
> and gave himself for me.[1]

I'll never forget those days. Seemed like we were all being crucified in one way or another. I loved David so much. He loved me and saw me as someone who was reliable, as somebody that would not walk out of his life forever. Somebody who would be always with him. Someone who would do anything for him.

David's love for me was precious. When I'm tempted to doubt my worth I always say, Jesus loves me. My family loves me. Sheila loves me. David loves me.

David's chemotherapy was scheduled for Monday. On Sunday night I went jogging for I was still playing Gaelic football and handball. I ran past the Church of Ireland just as the congregation were leaving the evening service. Our Protestant neighbour Florey Neill stopped me. She asked about David. She said they had a new rector called Ted Woods who believed in healing.

She asked, George, would you like to meet him?

I said, I would.

Entering a Protestant church in the Republic of Ireland in 1973 was a big step for a Catholic. Entering a Protestant church on a Sunday evening dressed as a jogger in a Gaelic jersey was an even bigger step. The neighbour introduced me to the minister and explained the situation. Within minutes Ted was on his knees on the church floor praying for David.

Afterwards he said, George, in the Church of Ireland we have a little healing service with the anointing of oil. I'd like to pray with David tomorrow before he goes into hospital if that's okay.

I said, I'd like that.

He said, You might mention it to your parish priest out of courtesy.

I said, I will.

We arranged that Ted would come and pray for David the following day, during my lunchtime break, before the afternoon chemotherapy session. Next morning after Mass I mentioned this to the parish priest.

I said, The Church of Ireland minister is coming down today to pray with David.

The parish priest became visibly uncomfortable. He

hemmed and he hawed. Then he said, I suppose it's all right as long as you don't believe in it.

David sat on Sheila's lap while Ted prayed and anointed David with oil. Afterwards Ted said, Sometimes death is the perfect healing.

Ted was the first person I'd ever heard say that. His words took some pressure off Sheila and me.

Within five minutes of Ted leaving there was a loud knock at our door. It was the parish priest. He also prayed for David. Catholics and Protestants praying in our home was a new thing.

Sometimes after chemotherapy David wouldn't feel too bad. Other times he'd be so sick his eyes would turn back in his head. I never mentioned this to Sheila.

I never blamed God. I sometimes wondered what it was like for God to watch His own son dying on the cross. David was a brave little boy. No whimpering or whining. Yet sometimes I'm haunted by the memories of his eyes turned back in his head.

One evening Sheila visited a friend. There was an electricity strike that night which left us without light or heat. I decided to put on a coal fire. We were out of firelighters and the sticks were damp. I struggled to start a blaze. David who was lying on the couch saw my predicament. He climbed off the couch and came to me kneeling in the dark and he put his head on my shoulder. He said, Poor old Da.

My usual practice was I'd go to early Mass and

David would stay in bed. Upon my return I'd hear him getting out of bed and coming down the stairs. When the door opened. I'd be waiting with my welcoming arms and he'd rush into them for a cuddle and hug.

One Wednesday I positioned myself inside the door. His footsteps were heavier than usual. Slowly the latch went up and the door opened. David stood there like a living corpse. He just managed to reach my arms before he vomited.

I put him back into bed, a bed from which he'd never again rise in his own strength. At night we only had candles and the fire. When David couldn't sleep I'd sit with him in the chair in front of the fire. In the morning I'd put him in beside Sheila and I'd try to get some rest myself. The doctor came on Saturday. She said David would be more comfortable in hospital.

I knew David would never return to our home again. I'd heard a quote from the Christian existentialist Gabriel Marcel. He said, *To say I love you is to say you'll never die.* In one of Marcel's plays a character declares, *To love a being is to say you, you in particular, will never die.*

This is a theme Marcel returns to again and again in his writing in his attempt to show the nature of the relationship between hope and love. Basically Marcel is saying, Because I love you, because I affirm you as being, there is something in you, which can bridge the abyss that I vaguely call death. He is saying, Love doesn't deny death rather love says death is not the end.

When I was carrying David downstairs for the very last time I stopped halfway and I said, David I love you.

Like Gabriel Marcel I was telling David he'd never die at least not in my heart. I then took him to the back window looking out onto green fields and the mountains. Again, I said, I love you David.

I carried him to the little red Sacred Heart light in our living room. Again I told him I loved him. I said, As long as that light is glowing there I'll always remember you. I walked out the door with him in my arms and as I did so the glass in the bottom of the door smashed behind me.

When we left the yard David said, Daddy, where are you taking me?

I said, I'm taking you to hospital. I will be with you all the time.

He was happy with that.

Even when facing death David was a determined little man. At one point when he was sleeping I thought I'd put some honey on his dry lips. The thought had hardly been formed before his hand shot out and he said, Daddy, don't want it.

I said to Sheila, I think he knows my mind.

My last memory of David alive is praying The *Our Father* with him. He was slipping in and out of sleep. He woke up and said, Daddy where's Mammy?

I said, Mammy's sleeping. She'll be here later.

As we started *The Our Father* I couldn't get beyond the first two words – Our Father.

I pondered, Our Father? Is He really my father? Is he really David's father? If so then he truly is *Our Father*, a loving father for both David and me.

When I thought like this some burden lifted. I left the hospital that night with a lightness to my step because I knew there was a Father in heaven who has taken our suffering and carried our sorrows.

I came back on Wednesday morning around 4:30am. I planned to stay most of the day. Sheila arrived around 6am. I left to go for a few hours sleep. No sooner had I put my head on the pillow than the phone rang.

It was Sheila. She said, Seoirse, you'd better come. There's a change taking place.

When I arrived back David was unconscious. A young doctor was trying to resuscitate him.

I silently prayed, Lord please don't revive our lovely little boy. He has suffered enough.

Shortly afterwards the nurse said, Your son has gone.

A LITTLE CHILD SHALL LEAD THEM

AFTER DAVID DIED, Sheila and I sat with him for a couple of hours talking. I loved Sheila. There was a strength in our relationship and a sweetness between us. The doctor said he'd be interested in exploring exactly what happened to David so we gave permission for an autopsy. We were to collect the body next afternoon.

The following morning was so disjointed. I missed David's welcoming eyes and our songs together.

When we came for the body the mortuary gates were locked. Quite a few cars from our home place accompanied us to help bring David home. Sheila and I were sitting on a wall waiting for the mortuary gate to open when a bus pulled up across the road.

Out of it stepped a man who walked into a shop, bought something and got back on the bus again. I was feeling unsure of the next part of my own journey but like the man on the bus I knew I'd get whatever I needed for the journey ahead.

Then the gate opened, the priest arrived, prayers were said and we headed for home in a low November sun, which for parts of the journey shone and sparkled on David's coffin.

As we travelled home, others joined our little cortège. On our way we met a wedding party with balloons flying and horns blaring reminding us that not everyone was sad that day. In the end there was a large cavalcade of us arriving into Milltown just as the pupils from my school were being let out. Hundreds of them surrounded us as we carried David into the Church of the Sacred Heart for the next day's funeral.

While shaving on the funeral morning I had a strong sense of déjà vu, a feeling of this being a moment I'd been preparing for all my life. I thought, There's a big job to be done and I'm ready for it. I'd made promises to David. I told him I loved him and I would never forget him.

I'd said, David I will do all the readings at your Mass. And wherever you're going to go I'm going to go before you as far as I possibly can. One day we will meet again in heaven.

So I went up to his open grave before Mass and I jumped into it and stood and prayed and praised God. Then I did a press up. I couldn't lie flat because I was wearing a suit. I felt I had gone as far as I physically could in fulfilling my commitment to David.

But in all my life, did I dream it? In my memory I always recall I was alone in the graveyard but Sheila insisted she was there with me. Maybe I was so focused on keeping my promise to David that nothing else seemed to register.

During mass we sang, *Suffer Little Children to Come unto Me* and *Give me Joy in my Heart keep me Singing.* I especially asked the choirmaster to sing, *Give me Joy.* In David's obituary I wanted the words *joyfully regretted* to be included in the death notice in the national paper.

Years later I discovered what we experienced then was actually very scriptural in the sense that joy is the reward one gets for recognising and accepting the divine deposit in every situation no matter how difficult. We weren't happy that David was dead but we still had joy. Sadness and joy can coexist.

Although we hadn't fully committed our lives to God at this point, we both felt God was teaching us there was a power higher than either of us, orchestrating our responses to the situation. By recognising that power and living in the provision of that power this thing called joy was our reward. Grief was leading us but joy was in our hearts.

When they placed David's little coffin in the grave I took the spade from the gravedigger and shovelled it all myself. The first shovel I more or less lashed into the grave. It ricocheted off the coffin. In some strange way I felt we were carrying the war to death. *Where O death is your victory? Where O death, is your sting?*

David was buried on Friday. On Sunday I togged out for the local Gaelic team. Before the kick off the opposing players lined up and shook my hand. Their full back in particular was very sympathetic. We then proceeded to belt the hell out of one another for the rest of the game. Football and being a part of the wider community helped ease Sheila and I back into everyday life after David's death.

I also got involved in training local GAA teams. If I had one strength in dressing rooms it was that I was focused. I never allowed deviation from the target. I made the main thing the main thing. We never gave up until the very end. We won a lot of games by one or two points.

I liked this because it meant we weren't giving in when times got difficult. And I don't remember ever been beaten by more than three or four points, which meant my own men were holding firm against the opposition.

I became a selector for the County Kerry under 21 team. At the time they were enjoying what became known as The Golden Years. At the beginning of these Golden Years one of the older selectors decided to retire from the locality, which meant there would be a vacancy in the senior selector's team. I was the automatic choice to take his place. But the Lord had other plans.

The team I was training was playing away and very soon into the game it became apparent to all present that the referee on that particular day was trying to produce a home win. He was less than fair to us. At the end of the match the crowd rushed the field.

Some were very angry and very verbal at the referee. I intervened and managed to drive the crowd back from the referee. There was lots of pushing and shoving. I then turned to the referee and expressed my own frustrations with his poor performance. Later I apologised to him.

Soon afterwards a letter dropped through my door. I'd been summoned before the County Board to give an account of myself. The referee reported I'd assaulted him.

I pondered what I should do. I knew a few phone calls to the right people would silence the whole affair but since David's death I wanted to do the right thing. I thought of Jesus saying, Whoever wants to save their life will lose it, but whoever loses their life for me will save it.[1]

So, I decided to let due process go ahead and I turned up before the general-purpose committee. The charge was read out and I was asked how I pleaded. I made no plea for mercy nor did I attempt to subvert the course of justice.

I said, The referee is an honourable man. If he says I'm not guilty then I'm not guilty. If he says I'm guilty then I'm guilty. He has said I'm guilty so then I plead, Guilty as charged!

I was given six months suspension. The knock on effect of this was I no longer automatically proceeded to become a senior selector. This meant I missed out being on the inside during the successful Golden Years.

But I'm sure this was all for the best because I could so easily have been carried away with all the success and celebration that I might have missed out on what God was doing in my life. I believe I got the better Golden Years in the end.

During David's illness we became friendly with Jack and Nelly Coleman, builders from Cork. Their son was a patient, not a cancer patient, in the same ward. One sunny afternoon I was playing with David while Sheila and Nelly were speaking.

I overheard Nelly say, I'm off now Sheila. I'm going to a prayer meeting. And with that she disappeared out the door. Her words piqued my curiosity. Prayer meeting?

My father was chairman of a cooperative creamery. Every month he chaired a creamery meeting. I was regularly at political meetings, teacher's meetings and football meetings. But I'd never in my life been to a prayer meeting.

In my mind the words prayer and meeting were

incompatible. If there was a meeting there'd be no prayer. When there was prayer there'd be no meeting. Yet for some reason the words prayer meeting penetrated deep into my thinking. When I later mentioned this to Sheila she had no memory whatsoever of this incident.

Five days after David's death I told Sheila I'd like to have a prayer meeting in our home with a few people. I wanted to read the Bible and see what sense was to be made of David's death. Sheila agreed with me. I invited Ted Woods and some folk from the Church of Ireland and some of my fellow teachers.

On November 19th 1973 twelve of us met in our front room for our first ever prayer meeting. I'd no idea what was supposed to happen. We read and discussed the Bible. Ted Woods was the only one of us who knew how to pray spontaneously in his own words.

We agreed to meet for ten weeks and if nothing of any significance happened by that time we'd just let it all go. I hadn't encountered charismatic renewal meetings at this time. There may have been some in Dublin or elsewhere but I'd never heard of them.

After ten weeks we just continued without further discussion for our meeting together was doing something good for all of us. From the outset I determined there'd be no easy way out. I didn't want to resort to formal prayers that I'd said thousands of times before.

I suppose I was seeking God in a new way, seeking

to really hear His voice. Looking for something alive and real. Something that was different because what had happened to us was different. David had died and our world had changed. We were looking for a real encounter with God.

From the very beginning of our prayer meetings I thought we should leave out an empty chair. This was a symbol of the presence of the Lord in our midst. We'd read from Matthew 18 where Jesus said, For where two or three gather together in My name, there am I with them.

Then as time passed I became obsessed with a problem caused by this chair. I thought, If Jesus is really present with us then why are we spending all our time talking about Him rather than talking to Him.

I shared this with the group. Some were disturbed at the prospect of actually talking to Jesus. Then one evening I risked my perceived respectability within the parish and my status as a teacher and actually started speaking to Jesus not as if He were present but on the basis that He was present.

Perspiration ran down my back and beads of sweat appeared on my face. This was a huge turning point in my spiritual life. I was acknowledging Jesus before men and He was acknowledging me before His Father in Heaven. A new door had opened but it was still a culture shock.

Our meetings have always been open to everyone,

Catholic, Protestant and Dissenter. We were never affiliated with the official Catholic Charismatic Organisation. Our meeting grew out of David's death. We've had continuous weekly meetings ever since. Well over forty years.

So in the end, *Something Beautiful for God* did emerge out of David's death. Our spiritual awakening and salvation really started with the death of our lovely son. From the word go I'd a sense we were not to let David's death be the end of anything but rather the beginning of something.

I determined Sheila and myself should not go back to business as usual and almost pretend David never existed. Instead his death opened a door into a new life for Sheila and me and many others. A huge transformation occurred in our worldview. We began to see things in a brand new way. The Bible became a fresh and living book.

When I first heard about charismatic meetings my mind was completely blown away at the idea that people were actually speaking in tongues like on the day of Pentecost. I remember thinking, If rowing a boat from Dublin to California would enable me to experience what the early Christians experienced I would gladly take on that task.

At our prayer meeting I began to talk about the possibility of us speaking in tongues but this was a bridge too far for some. Many didn't really expect the

Holy Spirit to manifest in our midst. The notion of Jesus in the chair was hard enough for them. I didn't know at the time how to cross that bridge but I knew I was going to find out.

God was doing a new thing in Ireland and I was going to be part of it. Saint Paul was converted on the road to Damascus and Saint Peter was converted again when Jesus cooked him fish on the beach and told him to feed his sheep. I was converted the year David died. Sheila and I came to a living personal faith in Jesus Christ that year. That's why we often said 1973 was the best year of our lives.

We started the weekly prayer meetings in our home a fortnight after David's burial. As the meetings continued we became more at ease with one another. Although we hadn't grown up in a culture where we'd normally share spiritual things, we grew to enjoy fellowshipping and talking about what Jesus meant to us.

At one meeting Ted Woods proposed we arrange a prayer meeting in the local community hall on Good Friday evening at a time when both congregations were leaving their respective churches.

This was a radical thing for 1974 Ireland, a revolutionary step in our town. Even though I'm normally a man under authority I never bothered asking the parish priest. Another priest friend of mine relayed to me a conversation he overheard between my parish priest and the Bishop.

My parish priest was complaining to the Bishop about the strange goings on at the prayer meeting at George McAuliffe's house every Thursday night. He asked the Bishop what he should do about it.

The Bishop said, In God's name, do nothing about it. Men and women praying together for their families, their communities and their nation is a very good thing. I only wish there were more people in Ireland doing that.

Before the Good Friday meeting a nun almost put a spanner in the works. Ted Woods was a great man for making small liturgy leaflets with a few scriptures and some words for every occasion. I had the leaflet printed out at the convent. One of the nuns decided to improve the liturgy and inserted a decade of the rosary after the scripture readings. Thank God for Tipp-Ex.

Around a hundred Catholics and Church of Ireland people came to that Good Friday meeting. Ted Woods and I were leading, but just before it officially started, when people were still finding their chairs, something extraordinary happened to me. It was as if I were taken over by an outside power for to my own surprise I stood up and I announced loudly that I was saved.

I kept saying, I am saved! I am saved! I am saved!

What Jesus did for me on the cross on that first

Good Friday hit me with such impact that the only response I had was to stand up and announce I was saved. Those were the only words that actively reflected what I understood and felt at that particular time.

So when people ask me when was I saved I reply I was saved on that First Good Friday when Jesus Christ died on Calvary's cross. But the penny really dropped in a big way for me on Good Friday 1974. I'd never heard the expression *I am saved*, before in my life. It was a most extraordinary thing for a man like myself to stand in front of a mixed congregation, some of them my own pupils, and tell them I was saved.

For three weeks in June 1973, I managed to say two thousand two hundred and fifty Hail Mary's each and every day. Fifteen Full Rosaries. In the Full Rosary there are the fifteen decades. Three fives of the Joyful Mysteries, the Sorrowful Mysteries and the Glorious Mysteries.

I was able to do this because I was supervising the Leaving Cert and most days I'd have six hours of silence during the exams. In those days the Rosary was the only way I knew how to pray. It was the only way I could express the desperation in my spirit as regards the situation of my dying son.

Once when I was summoned before the local Bishop for not honouring Mary at our meetings I mentioned this fact to him. The Bishop was a great Marian man.

I said, Bishop I don't say the Rosary at all nowadays.

I admire Mary. I respect Mary. I love Mary. I pray like Mary. Mary prayed in tongues and I pray in tongues. Mary prophesied and I prophesy. Mary told us to do whatever Jesus tells us to do. Jesus told us to pray always to the Father in Jesus' name. That's how I pray nowadays.

Of course I honour Mary. She is a great example to us all. Mary rejoiced in God her saviour and I rejoice in God my saviour. Mary kept holy and sacred things in her heart and I keep holy and sacred things in my heart. Mary is a wonderful example and a wonderful mother. She is a holy spiritual lady blessed amongst women who knew how to pray and prophesy and be filled with the Holy Spirit and incarnate Jesus to the world. She also knew how to suffer.

The Bishop was perturbed.

I said, Look Bishop if where I am today is wrong, isn't it awful poor reward I got for all these prayers I said to Mary?

Prior to the recent move of the Holy Spirit within the Catholic Church the Rosary was the main prayer of the Irish people. There wasn't much else for the common people.

We were a creedal church that said taught prayers rather than teaching people how to pray spontaneously to God in Jesus name. I've read somewhere that only 3% of Catholics have ever heard their father pray for them in a natural way.

My father never ever prayed or said the Rosary. My mother would make an attempt once every few years after the missionaries had been through. It might last for a night or two. I never said the Rosary as a boy. I never heard anybody say a spontaneous prayer until I met Ted Wood in 1973. Afterwards we began to pray from our hearts in our home prayer meeting.

The real miracle for me in my life was that love replaced anger and meaning replaced absurdities and joy replaced grief. These signs and wonders were the source that brought me to this point. It's really all about being obedient to Jesus. As Mary told the servants at the wedding feast of Cana, Do whatever he tells you.

I often think David like Mary had to suffer much. David paid a big price but his suffering and death opened the door for Sheila and I to come to a living faith and an intimate relationship with Jesus through his Holy Spirit.

Sheila always said 1973 was the best year of our lives, which sounds contradictory considering that was the year we lost our beautiful boy.

BAPTISM IN THE HOLY SPIRIT

TED WOODS occasionally invited me to meetings in his home. That's how I met the Rev Cecil Kerr in 1974, the year The Troubles in Northern Ireland claimed its 1,000th victim. Cecil was a gentle man and a great listener. He was lecturing at Queen's University Belfast at that time. Cecil was a Church of Ireland minister who'd recently been baptised in the Holy Spirit.

He then began meeting Catholics who'd also been baptised in the Holy Spirit. God was changing Cecil's theology and worldview much like St. Peter at Cornelius' house in Acts 10. The parallels were obvious, Jews didn't associate with Gentiles, Protestants didn't associate with Catholics. Peter told Cornelius, It's against our law for a Jew to associate with a Gentile but God has shown me I should not call anyone impure or unclean.

Peter was even more stunned when the Holy Spirit fell upon the Gentiles, and they began to speak in tongues and praise God. Peter's lifelong theology was changed by a single experience. The Gentiles had received the Holy Spirit the same way he and Jesus' disciples had.

When the apostles in Judea heard the Gentiles had received the word of God they were concerned. Peter calmed their fears. He said, If God gave them the same gift as He gave us when we believed on the Lord Jesus Christ who was I to withstand God?

Cecil Kerr was a modern-day St. Peter. When he realised Catholics were being baptised in the Holy Spirit and speaking in tongues and praising God, he accepted them as true believers. This led to him and his wife Myrtle founding the *Christian Renewal Centre* in Rostrevor, Northern Ireland in 1974. This centre was a place where Catholics and Protestants could fellowship and share their faith together. This was a revolutionary stance for its day.

In John 13 Jesus said, My children, a new command I give you: Love one another. As I have loved you, so you must love one another. By this everyone will know that you are my disciples, if you love one another.

If Christians, whatever their denomination, are just as alienated and superficial in their relationships with each other as everyone else then no amount of empty rhetoric or slick marketing will ever make up for it!

Nothing convinces unbelievers that God exists like the discovery of Christians who love one another.

The Holy Spirit always brings love, joy, peace, and unity. It happened in Acts 2 with the Jews, in Acts 8 with the Samaritans and in Acts 10 with the Gentiles.

Satan and his demons can't ever manifest love, joy, peace, and unity. They're always into strife and condemnation. Cecil Kerr's revelation and vision was that the Kingdom of God was a kingdom of love, joy and peace and that God is no respecter of persons but accepts from every nation the one who fears him and does what is right.

Ted Woods invited folk from our meeting to an event called *The New Wave of The Holy Spirit*. Only two of us Catholics were brave enough to attend. A couple of other Church of Ireland ministers were also in attendance. They were so unlike us. For the life of me I couldn't understand their theology. At the end of the meeting someone asked, Who would like to receive the Holy Spirit?

I raised my hand.

One of the Church of Ireland ministers prayed over me. He read Jesus' words from Luke 11, If you then, though you are evil, know how to give good gifts to your children, how much more will your Father in heaven give the Holy Spirit to those who ask him!

These words impacted me. I didn't speak in tongues but when I arrived home after midnight, I started reading the first lines of the *Acts of the Apostles* and I didn't stop until I reached the very end of the book. I was a thirsty cat lapping up fresh milk.

I saw that Jews, Samaritans and Gentiles all spoke in tongues and prophesied. The first Pope Peter spoke in tongues and prophesied, as did the rest of the apostles, as did Mary the mother of Jesus. She was in the upper room with the rest of the disciples when the promised Holy Spirit fell. Mary had already prophesied in Luke 1.

I was excited and delighted to think that what happened in the Book of Acts could be available to George and Sheila McAuliffe in Ireland in 1974.

Could it be true that Jesus was really the same yesterday today and forever? Was He still baptising people in His Holy Spirit?

THE CATHOLIC CHARISMATIC MOVEMENT.

SHEILA and I never heard of the Charismatic Movement until the end of 1974 or early 1975. It was possibly happening in Dublin or Cork but it hadn't got as far as Milltown. Then occasionally there'd be articles in the newspaper about how Catholics were being impacted by the Charismatic Movement.

In the summer of 1975 I went to my first Charismatic Conference in Dublin. There was tremendous excitement in the air. Thousands were singing and praying and praising in tongues. At one point I raised my hands and said, Okay Lord, here goes, tongues or burst. And immediately out of my mouth poured a river of words I'd never learned.

It wasn't a language I already knew like Irish or English or High Level Latin. It was a new heavenly language. That was another major turning point in my life with God. I received a great excitement from the Charismatic Movement. I was so blessed that Jesus was alive and joy was our portion.

I came across a little book called *The Power of Praise* by Merlin R Carothers. It opened up my spirit to praising God in all circumstances. Apart from the Bible that was my favourite book for many years.

Before I read this book I thought one has to be good at English in order to pray well. But then I realised praise was very simple. You don't have to be a scholar to praise or thank God and you certainly you don't have to be a scholar to get excited and dance.

For me the power of praise was the key that unlocked everything else. All that came with the Charismatic Movement. The power of praise was the key to me.

I remember hearing the Belfast worship leader Jackie McArthur teaching on praise. He said, Praise penetrates through the powers and principalities of the air into the presence of God and worship is what we do when we get there.

Those words were music to my ears. I see worship as the final destination of our journey to God. You can't worship God and be depressed at the same time.

The speakers at that 1975 Charismatic Conference were the Rev Tom Smail, Cardinal Suenens and the Rev Cecil Kerr. The audience included Northerners, Southerners, Unionists, Republicans, Protestants and Catholics.

Cardinal Suenens said if we have unity with Jesus then we will be united with one another. He said we should be patiently impatient for unity.

Cecil Kerr said we were the most representative body of Christians from every part of Ireland that had ever met in this land. Cecil also told us to look unto Jesus. He quoted from John 12 where Jesus said; If I be lifted up I will draw all men onto me.

Cecil said we were not drawn to a denomination, a fellowship or some new wind of doctrine but to Jesus Christ and as we are drawn to Him we will also be drawn to one another. Jesus' last prayer on earth was for unity. The people heartily responded to Cecil's talk. They gave him a standing ovation.

In the evening meeting the leader of the Charismatic Community in Dublin said something that alarmed and dismayed me. He said the leadership committee planned to go on a weekend retreat in order to discern God's will for the movement.

My heart sank. I thought if they hadn't already discerned God's plan for the movement in the words of Cecil Kerr in the morning meeting how on earth were they ever going to discern it. I thought of Isaiah 42,

Hear, you deaf; look, you blind, and see!

Who is blind but my servant, and deaf like
    the messenger I send?
Who is blind like the one in covenant
    with me,
Blind like the servant of the Lord?
You have seen many things, but you pay
    no attention;
Your ears are open, but you do not listen.

The result of their time away was that they began calling themselves the *Catholic Charismatic Movement.* This was the very sectarian spirit Cecil Kerr had warned us against.

I suppose if the Pope and his cardinals had ex cathedra come up with a new movement including the baptism of the Holy Spirit and the gifts of the Holy Spirit they then might have been justified in calling it the *Catholic Charismatic Movement.*

But the wind of change then blowing throughout the world and through me personally was not something created by man. It was a sovereign work of God. You could no more have a Catholic Charismatic Movement than a Catholic flu, a Catholic wind or a Catholic thunderstorm.

I joyfully received the gift of tongues at that conference and while I couldn't help but rejoice at some of the content I became very concerned about the barricade they were creating around it. Were they trying to quarantine the move of the Holy Spirit within the Catholic Church before it really got going?

Scripture says the wind blows where it wants to and so is every man who is born of the Spirit.[1] Did thy think they could contain the wind and direct it to blow only amongst Catholic people? How foolish is that? I am still part of the Catholic Charismatic Movement but I don't agree with the sectarian direction it took.

In 1974, when Catholics and Protestants came together in Dublin for the First National Irish Charismatic Conference, Ireland became the only country in the world where the Catholic National Service Committee included Protestant members.

This was a prophetic sign, in light of war torn Northern Ireland. Unfortunately, a few years later the Protestants were asked to leave for fear their involvement might jeopardise the Catholic Church's approval of the movement.

Gradually the Protestant wing of the charismatic movement began to be marginalised in Ireland. This reduced the prophetic challenges of the renewal and weakened its biblical grounding. It sucked the life out of it. This was very sad because the Charismatic conference was the only conference for donkey's years to gather Catholics and Protestants together.

There was still occasional lip service about Christian unity but it wasn't real. I remember Tom Smail saying, Christian unity is not Rome talking to Canterbury and Canterbury talking to Constantinople and Moscow talking to Rome. It's about all of us speaking to Jesus Christ. Tom's version of Christian unity appealed to me.

Catholic fear towards Protestants caused this withdrawal. The early excitement and energy of the movement was waning. The leadership didn't know how to deal with Holy Spirit freedom. Instead fear hijacked the movement and funnelled it into a narrow channel that suited the Catholic Church but left us all spiritually poorer.

We lost the unity and the liberty of the Holy Spirit. I'd wanted to be part of breaking down of the walls of division rather than supporting the control and chains of men.

There used to be a joke about a Russian atheist showing a poster of an Irish riot and saying, Look how those Christian's love one another. The joke wasn't too far from the truth. My people and I had been too long a part of that hatred. I now wanted to be part of the love.

In 1959 Pope John XXIII at the sudden inspiration of the Holy Spirit called for the first ecumenical council for the Roman Catholic Church. This was only the third council since the Reformation. An important aspect of the council was the fostering of Christian unity. In Ireland through fear we began to lose sight of this necessary ingredient of unity. This resulted in a complete loss of prophetic significance and a sad return to orthodoxy and piety. God's intentions for the renewal were badly thwarted.

Thank God for the present Pope Francis. He offers new hope for the Catholic Church. In an interview in the Italian newspaper *La Repubblica* he took a swipe at the hierarchy by condemning its Vatican-centric view.

He said, I believe in God, not in a Catholic God. There is no Catholic God, there is only God and I believe in Jesus Christ, his incarnation. Jesus is my teacher and my pastor but God, the Father, Abba, is the light and the Creator.

He said, A Vatican-centric view neglects the world around us.

He also said, I do not share this view, and I'll do everything I can to change it. The Church is or should go back to being a community of God's people, and priests, pastors and bishops who have the care of souls and are at the service of the people of God.

Unfortunately Pope Francis wasn't around in 1975.

THE FULL GOSPEL BUSINESSMEN

I FIRST HEARD about *The Full Gospel Businessmen* from Pascal Coffey, a fellow teacher in the late 1970s. Pascal said, George there's a crowd doing the rounds called *The Full Gospel Businessmen*. They're very Protestant I hear.

I said, Tell me more.

Pascal said, Their official title is the Full Gospel Business Men's Fellowship International or FGBMFI for short.

I said, By God that's a mouthful even for a man like yourself.

Pascal explained the Full Gospel Businessmen were comprised of Christians from various denominations and working backgrounds. Catholics, Protestants and Dissenters he said, appealing to my Republican heritage.

He said they met in hotels and that everyone was welcome, male and female. He also mentioned they prayed for the baptism in the Holy Spirit and for healing and they believed in miracles.

I didn't know whether I was being warned off or not but the more Pascal described them the more attractive they appeared. They were experiencing the same things as us yet they were coming from the very crowd I wanted to kill at one time. My heart was opening to them.

A couple of years later I walked into our living room in Kilcolman, where Sheila was watching *The Late Late Show with Gay Byrne*. Gay was interviewing two Full Gospel Businessmen. One was Al Ryan, a Republic of Ireland Catholic and an ex IRA soldier who'd served time for his political beliefs. The other was Hector Crory, a Protestant businessman from the Unionist community in the North of Ireland.

I stood watching the interview. What they said resonated with me. Politically and religiously they were poles apart yet they found agreement in the name of Jesus Christ and in the baptism of the Holy Spirit. That got my attention.

But the next thing got my attention even more. A voice in my spirit spoke to me.

The voice said, One day you will be part of that fellowship.

The voice also said, Al Ryan has a message for you.

As I stood watching the television these words registered deeply within me, One day you'll be part of that fellowship and Al Ryan has a message for you. I never mentioned these two revelations to Sheila or anyone else.

Like Mother Mary I kept them in my heart. I also did nothing whatsoever to make these things happen. I didn't try to contact the Full Gospel Businessmen or Al Ryan. I believed if a supernatural word or a prophecy was going to happen then it was going to happen without any assistance from me.

Three years later I returned from a round of golf and walked into the same living room. Two strangers were sitting drinking tea with Sheila. Sheila said, Seóirse, this is Mike and Angela Frawley from Co. Galway. God told Angela she'd meet a man called George in Co. Kerry.

I was immediately sceptical. We shook hands.

Normally I'm doubtful about people and I don't take anyone at face value. Hosting open prayer meetings for many years has helped to make me that way.

Angela said they were moving from Galway to Killarney where she'd a new job. She again said God had told her she'd meet a man called George in Co. Kerry.

If what she said was a prophecy then I was disobedient to what St Paul said in 1 Thessalonians 5:20 where he warned us not to despise prophesy. Not only did I despise her words, I totally dismissed them. I wasn't at all sure about this couple but just as they were about to leave I said, I haven't a clue why you're here but for some reason the words Full Gospel keeps coming to mind.

Mike became excited. He said he knew Charles Lamb the president of the Full Gospel Businessmen's Fellowship in Ireland.

We shook hands and they left.

A couple of weeks later in June 1983 I got a phone call from Gerry Farrell from Dublin. Gerry said Mike Frawley had told him I was interested in the Full Gospel Businessmen and could we get together for a cup of coffee.

It was arranged Gerry and Mike and I would meet up in Killarney. In the end Mike couldn't make it so Sheila came instead. Gerry brought his wife. I thought we were meeting for information, only to discover Gerry wanted us to host the first Full Gospel Business-men's meeting in Co. Kerry.

Gerry was persuasive. Although I've no talent whatsoever for organising these things we agreed and scheduled a mini convention for October 1983 at a nearby hotel. The Full Gospel people would provide speakers etc. I felt out of my depth.

Vincent was Sheila's brother-in-law. Although Vincent and I were married to two sisters there was no great love lost between us. Vincent felt important enough to term me a culchie.

Vincent had suffered from Parkinson's disease and depression for over ten years. He was addicted to cigarettes and alcohol. When Sheila and I would visit, Vincent would quickly disappear from the room muttering things about culchies under his breath.

I'd occasionally invite Vincent to our prayer meeting but he always refused point-blank.

He was blunt. He'd say, I want nothing whatsoever to do with the insanity of the Charismatic Movement.

The evening before the mini convention Sheila and I visited Vincent and his wife. They was watching a television program about the greatest heroes of the Bible. The character been presented was King David.

I said, Vincent there's a meeting in the local hotel tomorrow night. Would you come to it?

I will, he said.

You could have knocked me down with a feather. It was arranged Sheila would take Vincent to the meeting.

I'd expected a couple of dozen people to turn up but there were well over two hundred people in attendance, a crowd from the North of Ireland and a shower from our county. I was leading the first session.

I'd never been to a Full Gospel meeting in my life so I'd no idea of the format or protocol. I hadn't the faintest idea of what to do but that never stopped me before. I stood up and said, Ladies and gentlemen, brothers and sisters, you are looking at and listening to a man who doesn't know what to say next.

That was exactly my situation. I could have started talking about the green glens of Antrim or Ireland's ancient mythological heroes. I hadn't the faintest inkling what to say next. Just then a bolt of power about the size of my fist hit me in the top of my head and smashed right down through my body into my feet. I staggered to keep balance.

Afterwards the difficulty was not in getting me to speak but in shutting me up. Later some people said they actually saw the jolt and felt the spiritual change. A Full Gospel leader from Castlederg called Thomas Kane was sitting beside Sheila when he saw something happening.

He asked her, Do you know that man leading that meeting.

Sheila said, I do actually. He's my husband.

The result was a definite energy from above. This new power enabled me to give a direction to the meeting and focus on the finished work of Jesus Christ on Calvary. From that moment on the entire convention flowed effortlessly. I felt peace and at ease about the whole thing.

The meeting room was visible from the foyer of the hotel. When Sheila and Vincent first entered they spied me speaking up in front of the crowd.

Vincent said, In the name of God, what's that idiot

doing above there?

Vincent immediately decided against attending my meeting. Instead Sheila took him up to a bedroom to be prayed for by Basil Donnelly of the famous Donnelly's Sausages family. Basil had been a rip roaring alcoholic in his day. He used to say he fought on both sides in the Greek Civil War when he was in the British Army. Basil was one of the main speakers at that conference.

Basil prayed with Vincent who was immediately slain in the spirit and fell on to the bed. Vincent's packet of twenty cigarettes was sticking out of his pocket. Basil took the cigarettes and put them to one side. After a while Vincent recovered and Sheila took him home.

From that day to the day he died thirty years later Vincent never smoked another cigarette, nor ever again drank alcohol. He rarely left the Bible out of his hand. Day and night he'd have the word of God in his hand and in his mouth. Vincent prayed without ceasing and was constantly praising the Lord.

Vincent went into that hotel one way and came out another. He was a new man. He went in calling me an idiot and he came out almost genuflecting in front of me. His whole attitude towards me changed. He became one of my greatest supporters. He was always at our meeting and travelled all over Ireland with me sharing his testimony. Previously he wasn't able to travel in a car because of his illness.

Vincent who'd won an All Ireland GAA football medal in his youth became a sign and a wonder in the community and though he still had Parkinson's he was a totally different human being. Instead of depression he had joy. He was a great singer. He delighted in praising the Lord. His story and testimony became well known throughout Ireland. He was a dynamo for the Lord. This was the result of just one prayer.

The Full Gospel Businessmen were presented to me as a fellowship where people could receive the baptism of the Holy Spirit and a joyful appreciation of the reality of Jesus Christ in their lives.

And if this experience wasn't already happening in their own church they should stay there and witness to it. And if it was happening in their own church they should stay there and enjoy it and help others grow into an awareness of it. There was never any sense of, *Come out from among them and join us,* never any suggestion of sheep stealing.

God led me to the Full Gospel Fellowship and confirmed this calling to me with signs following. I've often said, If God wanted me to be involved in the promotion of the Miraculous Medal he'd have seen to it that I had great experiences through the Miraculous Medal. He would have convinced me through my experiences of the Miraculous Medal that here was something everyone should become involved with.

He most definitively convinced me through experience, that the Full Gospel Businessmen Fellowship, was a God ordained ministry of blessing to the people of Ireland.

The wheels were turning. A year after Vincent's healing we started regular Full Gospel monthly meetings. Al Ryan the ex IRA prisoner was the main speaker at the first meeting. I remember the voice had said, Al had a message for me. I was curious to know just what that message might be. Al and I came from similar backgrounds so he was easy to relate to.

In prison Al kept hearing a voice that told him to, *Keep the peace.* On the morning he was released to his wife Peggy he heard it for one last time.

As the prison doors banged shut behind him the voice again said, *Remember Al. Keep the peace!*

At the end of first meeting I took Al, aside and said, Al you have a message for me.

He said, I have indeed George.

And what is it?

He said, This morning, God gave me a vision of you with a little boy in your arms. At one point you placed the little boy at the feet of the Lord. Then I saw the little boy dancing with joy before the Lord. Does that make any sense to you?

I said, It makes lots of sense.

Al didn't know we'd lost David ten years earlier.

SIGNS AND WONDERS

AT THE SECOND Full Gospel meeting in our county I was under fierce pressure. The musicians hadn't turned up, there weren't enough song sheets and I had to lead the worship myself. Our two guest speakers, a priest and Basil Donnelly were not hitting it off.

The priest who'd imbibed a little too much whiskey over dinner was bad mouthing Born Again Christians. Basil was a Born Again Christian and I was piggy in the middle. Basil wouldn't be drawn into an argument. His only reply to the priest was, Let's keep our eyes upon Jesus!

The priest was our main speaker. His topic was, *The Feminisation of the Catholic Church through the Blessed Virgin Mary.* I couldn't understand a word of it. Then Basil prayed for the sick and there was some commotion. I was so relieved when it was all over. Sheila and I arrived home exhausted long after midnight.

We were dismayed to find the priest and another man sitting in our kitchen. The priest was livid. Seemed like smoke was coming out of his nostrils. And it wasn't holy smoke.

Both men started tearing the meeting apart. This was wrong, that was wrong. Who does Basil Donnelly think he is? How dare he say that! Blah, blah, blah, on and on it went. And just before they left the priest fired his parting shot. He'd kept the best wine until the last. I can still hear his shrill and angry voice.

He said, And furthermore that poor girl dressed in black was visibly distressed by her experience inside there tonight.

I looked at Sheila. Afterwards I said, What in the name of God have we let loose in Ireland?

We went off to bed with heavy hearts.

Next morning at 7.30am our phone rang. It was a man from last night's meeting.

He said, George there's a young lady here called Margaret Wade who wants to speak to you. Is that okay?

I said, Of course it is.

Margaret was excited. She said, George you don't know me but I was at the meeting last night. I was dressed in black near the front. I've been very sick. I've an inoperable tumour on my brain. Three months ago the doctors give me six months to live. I'm exhausted all the time.

For the last fortnight I haven't been able to eat a single thing. But last night when that man Basil Donnelly prayed for me I immediately felt better but I didn't know what to do or say. But afterwards in the car park I couldn't contain myself. I was overjoyed. I felt so full of life.

Then my husband and I and some of the Full Gospel men came back to our home in and cooked a big fry of bacon, sausage and eggs and I was able to eat to my heart's content. I didn't sleep much last night. I'm so excited. I couldn't wait any longer without telling others about my healing. I hope you don't mind me ringing so early.

I said, Praise the Lord Margaret! I don't mind at all!

Isn't God good? His ways are not our ways. The very girl the priest focused on to demonise our meeting was the very person Jesus healed of a brain tumour.

Eleven years later to the day I was sharing my testimony at another Full Gospel meeting. Margaret and her husband had now moved to another county.

I said to Sheila, I'm giving my testimony tonight. It's been eleven years since Margaret Wade was healed. Is there any chance you might be able to trace her?

Sheila was excellent at this sort of thing. She had Margaret on the phone in no time.

I said, Margaret I want you to tell me again what exactly happened that night eleven years ago.

And Margaret told it all again, the very same story as the first time. Basil prayed for her, something left her and she had been in excellent health ever since. She had even got her medical records from the hospital.

The doctor said, So you had the operation after all?

Margaret said, I had an operation but it was from the Holy Spirit. He didn't have to use a knife.

Margaret and her family were still going on with the Lord hosting a weekly meeting in their home.

Thirty years after the night Margaret was healed I happened to be at a college event when I met the disgruntled priest from that second Full Gospel meeting.

I said, Father I want to give you the phone number of a girl who has a story for you. So I give him Margaret Wade's phone number. I don't know if he ever rang her or not.

Cliff de Gersigny was a sign and a wonder. I really loved this man. Cliff was a white South African businessman, a director of thirty-two companies. He was the main speaker at our third Full Gospel meetings. Cliff and I were Catholics who'd come to a strong faith in Jesus Christ in the 1970s.

Cliff became Catholic Archbishop Denis Hurley's right-hand man in South Africa. Cliff had a gift of miracles. I've seen more miracles through Cliff's ministry than I ever thought possible.

Cliff appeared in our town one Friday afternoon in 1984 and was immediately put to work. That night we'd a meeting in our home. The local curate and a dozen people including Pat Healy and Pa Herron were there. Pat had a bad back. The doctors said he was heading towards a wheelchair.

Cliff preached about the resurrection of Jesus Christ. He was as bold as a lion. He claimed Jesus was still alive and was the same yesterday, today and forever. He quoted from 1 John 3, The reason the Son of God appeared was to destroy the devil's work.

He roared, Sickness is the Devil's work. Jesus healed the sick and told us to do the same.

He quoted from Acts 10, about how God anointed Jesus of Nazareth with the Holy Spirit and power, and how he went around doing good and healing all who were under the power of the devil, because God was with him.

At the end of the meeting we were all overawed by Cliff's eloquence and audacity. There was total silence. Cliff straightened up and looked around the room. He said, Well has anybody got anything to say?

I was about to say, Well Cliff we generally have a cup of tea about this time but I thought the better of it. Instead I said, Actually Cliff, I've had a recurring pain in my back for a few years. At night I'll sleep for about four hours then I have to walk around for an hour or so to relieve the pain. I haven't had a full night's sleep for donkey's years. I've also developed a kind of gait, a shuffle, to accommodate this pain.

Cliff seated me on a chair with my back against the wall. He asked me to lift up my feet, which he rested in his hands. He pointed out that one leg was shorter than the other. We could all see this. He called the people to come and watch. The curate leaned in closest. And then he declared, Be healed in Jesus' name!

Immediately my leg lengthened.

He placed his hands upon my back and told it also to be healed in Jesus' name. He told me to stand up. I was uncomfortable because my balance had changed but the pain had gone and it never came back. I've slept like a baby ever since.

Cliff said, Anyone else needs healing?

Pat Healy volunteered his bad back. Cliff repeated the process. Pat's short leg inched out and he was instantly healed. A couple of days later he drove to Dublin through Wexford to the All Ireland Final without the slightest discomfort. Jesus had destroyed another work of the Devil.

Pa Heron's bad back was affecting his work as a lorry driver. He was also instantly healed.

A week later we had another meeting with Cliff.

Cliff asked, How's your back Pa?

Pa said, My back's fine but my hip is bothering me a bit.

Okay, said Cliff, Let's deal with that.

Clifford prayed, Be healed in Jesus' name.

Pa's hip was perfectly restored.

With Cliff the proof of the pudding was always in the eating.

At one of our meetings Cliff lifted a jug of water and started pouring it into a glass. He put in a little water. Then he filled the glass. Then he overflowed the glass.

He said the water represented the Holy Spirit. He said we didn't need just a little of the Holy Spirit in us. We didn't just need to be filled with the Holy Spirit. We needed to be overflowing with the Holy Spirit. As the water cascaded onto the table his point was well made.

At at large Full Gospel Meeting we were worshipping God with hands raised. I was back in the main body of people and Cliff was at the top table beside the musicians. I was wearing a suit. Suddenly a rushing wind blew into my back and kept blowing. My suit jacket was fluttering. I couldn't believe this was happening.

I was being propelled forwards and I started to lean backwards. I rested against the wind for a while before I was knocked to the floor. I stood up and tried to maintain my position but I was forcefully propelled forward by this wind until I finished up beside Cliff at the main speaker's table.

This experience was so out of the ordinary to me that I have to remind my self I am not a fool. In the past had I heard any man speaking as I'm speaking now I would have ridiculed it as being a complete delusion. But I know I wasn't deluded. My reputation might be that of a man with a penchant for recklessness but definitely not one of a man with a proclivity for fantasies.

I've often pondered about this rushing wind experience. Perhaps the Lord wanted me to align myself a little more with Cliff's ministry. Certainly a connection was made. Cliff had a huge burden for the people in the North of Ireland. I made arrangements with George Allen, a Full Gospel leader, who made available his cottage in Portadown as a base from which we ministered all over the north including a day in Long Kesh prison.

By this time the Holy Spirit had become more than just a doctrine to Sheila and me. We had moved from discussing about Jesus, to talking to Jesus, to daily experiencing Jesus working through his Holy Spirit. Seemed like Jesus had gotten out of that empty chair in my front room and was walking amongst us.

One day after school the parish priest was waiting for me

He said, George may I have a word with you?

Certainly Father.

He said, George, do you know anything about a little finger being replaced?

I said, Father you have finally come to the right man. Not only do I know about a little finger being replaced. I was there when the little finger was replaced. Why are you asking?

He told me the priests of the diocese had a meeting with Bishop Murphy, the Bishop of Kerry, a few weeks previously. Bishop Murphy explained he'd received an official letter from South Africa's Archbishop Denis Hurley requesting an investigation and some kind of proof about a claim made by Cliff de Gersigny for the miracle of a new finger being replaced on a young man from the Co. Kerry.

Since then the local priests were asking all around to try and get to the bottom of this.

I suspected I was probably the last man to be asked, the last man my parish priest would want to credit with having any connection whatsoever with a miracle.

What happened was this. Cliff and his wife Jen were staying with us and we arranged a healing service at a local convent. Cliff was laying hands on the people and I was standing beside him directing the prayer line. A young man in his late twenties, with a little tremor in his voice, asked for prayer.

He said to Cliff, Would the Lord be able to do anything for my little finger? When I was four years old it got crushed in a door and it has never developed beyond this stub. As you can see it has now turned in under the next finger and is causing me trouble at work.

Cliff said, Okay let's see!

Cliff prayed, Be healed in Jesus' name!

Within twenty seconds we were looking at a brand new finger. It was a little slighter and cleaner then the other little finger on the right hand.

I didn't know what to think. I knew I was in the presence of God. I was as certain about that new finger as I was certain that I saw my son David in his coffin. I can't be more certain than that.

Cliff took a photograph of the new finger. He showed this photograph at a meeting in South Africa and testified to how this finger was instantly replaced. Archbishop Denis Hurley heard a tape of this service and as a Catholic leader required proof before he could declare it to be a miracle.

So I got the young man to write out his testimony of the new finger. His parents also wrote their account of the new finger. Their parish priest also wrote a letter witnessing to the fact that the man with the new finger came from a decent trustworthy Catholic family. I sent the whole lot over to Archbishop Denis Hurley.

Cliff at this stage had left the Catholic Church but not in the bad sense of walking away in anger. There was just no opportunity for him to move in his Holy Spirit gifts within the Catholic Church at that time.

Archbishop Hurley realised the Catholic Church

was not yet ready for Cliff's ministry. Doors were closed because of clerical unbelief. So the Archbishop blessed and released Cliff to minister to the whole church and the whole world. That's how Cliff came to be in our county.

I wonder just how many more Catholics like Cliff will have to walk the same lonely road before the clerics within the Catholic Church will allow Pope John XXIII's prayer for a New Pentecost to come to pass?

GOLDEN DAYS

CLIFF DE GERSIGNY caused an explosion of numbers in our weekly home meeting. People experienced the Holy Spirit and wanted more. A new group from Alcoholics Anonymous joined us. Isaiah 55 was their favourite scripture,

> Come, all you who are thirsty, come to the
> waters; and you who have no money,
> come, buy and eat! Come, buy wine
> and milk without money and without
> cost.

Sometimes our meetings lasted until dawn. Later the National Full Gospel Convention was held nearby and another chapter was formed. One time our usual hotel room wasn't available so the management put us into the bar. There were about eight alcoholics in our group. One of them said he remembered a time when if they'd been left alone in a bar like this the top shelf would have been empty by now and they'd all have been *very full* gospel businessmen.

Full Gospel meetings were always an experience. It was always encouraging and inspiring to hear how God was working in ordinary people's lives. We overcame Satan by the blood of the lamb and the power of our testimony.

Full Gospel meetings weren't just about teaching and preaching. There was usually a tangible demonstration of the presence and power of the Holy Spirit. People were healed. People were delivered. Miracles happened. Prayers were answered.

God was alive and well in our midst. Jesus was the same yesterday today and forever. It was not just a ritual. We were constantly experiencing God in brand new ways.

Occasionally someone would say something like, George you've been lucky because you have seen so many signs and wonders over the years.

My reply is always along the lines of, Yes, I have seen signs and wonders but I didn't set out to see signs and wonders. I didn't go looking for signs and wonders. At the beginning all I saw was a brave little boy struggling with cancer and a loving mother holding her first son's pale hands praying for a miracle.

I also saw a family home unfinished because of a lack of finance. We didn't even have a proper bed for the children, two of them slept on a mattress on the floor. A wheelbarrow of sand in the midst of rubble was their playground. There were debts and doubts and no signs and wonders in those early days.

Our County Kerry Gaelic team had their Golden Days and sometimes I think of the Golden Days of the Holy Spirit in County Kerry. The beginning was exciting and exhilarating, full of heady hope and promise. A new wind of the Holy Spirit was sweeping the land and Acts 29 was taking place in Ireland.

Then over time things and people became subdued and controlled. I've heard it said, Every new move of God begins with a prophet and ends with a policeman. I don't want to sound critical but a recurring theme from Catholic circles about the proof of the authenticity of the Charismatic Movement was the fact that Mary was always pointed to by the Holy Spirit.

I love and respect Mary. She's a wonderful example of a humble handmaiden of the Lord who interceded, prophesied, spoke in tongues and walked in obedient faith. She's an amazing example for all of us but in the Bible it is always Jesus that is being exalted by the Holy Spirit. In John 15:26 Jesus said, I will send you the Advocate, the Spirit of truth. He will come to you from the Father and will testify all about me.

The Holy Spirit is always testifying and pointing to

Jesus. We have lost our way when we try to squeeze new wine into old wineskins. Joy is then robbed of its vitality and excitement. Of course God still works. He works all things together for good. He knows what He is doing. He hasn't yet finished with Ireland.

If it hadn't been for the Full Gospel Businessmen's Fellowship, Sheila and I would have been left in a spiritual backwater. For us the Full Gospel Businessmen was a connection to the wider church and a bigger vision of what the Holy Spirit was doing all over the world.

This was not just confined to Co. Kerry or the Catholic Church. We know the Holy Spirit is being poured out upon all people all over the globe right now. We know the earth will be filled with the glory of God as the waters cover the sea. We know God will have his way in Ireland despite the current bleakness of the spiritual landscape.

Acts 2 says,

> In the last days, God says, I will pour out
> my Spirit on all people. Your sons and
> daughters will prophesy, your young
> men will see visions, your old men will
> dream dreams. Even on my servants,
> both men and women, I will pour out
> my Spirit in those days, and they will
> prophesy.

I believe the fullness of what God intended for the Catholic Church through the Charismatic Movement has not yet happened. Many people who were deeply touched by the Holy Spirit have been displaced from the Catholic Church. Others have been quarantined and bored to death by irrelevant homilies. Yet the reality is 1.2 billion Catholics are not going to leave their Church and join Protestant denominations anytime in the near future.

THE BEST IS YET TO COME

THE *FULL GOSPEL Business Men's Fellowship International* started from a vision God gave to an Armenian dairyman from California, called Demos Shakarian. In the early 1950s Demos came to the prophetic under-standing we are presently living in a time when one of the most major events foretold in the Bible is taking place.

We are living in the period just before Jesus returns to earth. We are living at a point in God's plans and purpose when Jesus is pouring his Holy Spirit out upon all people all over the world. Not just upon Catholics, Protestants, Pentecostals, Russian Orthodox, Quakers, Baptists, Greek Orthodox and so on but upon all flesh, all mankind.

I have no doubt about this vision. If we only listen to the media it appears Christianity is a beaten docket, all doom and gloom. The real truth is far from that. Isaiah 11:9 says, The earth shall be full of the knowledge of the Lord as the waters cover the sea.

Habakkuk 2:14 says, For the earth will be filled with the knowledge of the glory of the Lord as the waters cover the sea. Numbers 14:21 also says, Truly, as I live, all the earth shall be filled with the glory of the Lord.

Today, as Demos realised, the full gospel of Jesus Christ is being preached all over the world and His Holy Spirit is being poured out upon all people. Christianity is exploding with more than 200,000 people becoming new believers every single day, over 20,000 per day in China and over 35,000 per day in South America alone.

Some of us sometimes wish we were back in the days of the early church when three thousand people were saved on the day of Pentecost. What power! What amazing growth! Today 3,000 people are being saved every 25 minutes. Imagine that! The day of Pentecost repeating itself every half hour.

Research shows that Pentecostals and Charismatics now make up more than a quarter of all Christians. They also make up more than 8% of the world's total population. Nowadays half of the world's Pentecostals and Charismatics live in sub-Saharan Africa.

In 1952, God told Demos to start a Fellowship for men who would meet in small and large groups in cafes, hotels and public places to fellowship and minister spiritually one to another. Part of Demos' call was to release men into a life of faith.

His call was to equip ordinary working people who knew and loved the Lord and just didn't know how to express it. Men who were willing to tell one another what they had experienced of God in their lives. Men who might not believe what a priest or a preacher might say but who would listen to a schoolteacher, a plumber or a motor mechanic because they were a schoolteacher, a plumber, or a motor mechanic themselves.

It was called *Full Gospel* because no biblical subject would be avoided at the meetings. Healing. Speaking in tongues. Prophecy. Miracles. Deliverance. Whatever a man's experience, he could talk about it just as it happened. Ordinary men could speak about what God was doing in their lives and families and workplace.

It was called *Business Men* because it was comprised of laymen, ordinary people. It was called *Fellowship* because it was just a bunch of people who loved to get together and share about Jesus in their lives. It was not to be a rules and committees and a meeting-come-to-order event.

It was called *International* because it was for all men from all nations.

One thing I particularly found attractive about the Full Gospel Businessmen was their non-sectarian spirit. When I first heard Al Ryan and Hector Crory on

The Gay Byrne Show they said their mission was to encourage people into a living relationship with Jesus Christ and being filled with His Holy Spirit and operating in the gifts and power of His Holy Spirit.

These people would then go back into their own particular church, denomination or fellowship and bring the good news of their experience of the Holy Spirit back to base. I'm convinced this strategy was tailor made for the Irish situation.

Nothing gives me greater joy than sharing fellowship with brothers and sisters in Christ from different denominations without me harbouring a secret hope that I'm going to make a Catholic out of them.

And I hope the same freedom is enjoyed by believers from Protestant backgrounds. They don't have to be under pressure to persuade me to come out from among the Catholics and become some variety of a Protestant. How sad that would be.

The Full Gospel Fellowship encouraged people to remain in their own churches and be a witness there of their new life in the Holy Spirit. I thought of what this might look like.

I imagined that I was sick in hospital and because of proper care I was made well. I was now at a stage where I could leave hospital but I could also be called back into hospital to share the secret of my health with other patients so they too could get better.

I wouldn't be doing much good by going back into

hospital and agreeing to be sick again just so that I wouldn't upset the rest of the people in the hospital. Nor would I satisfy the requirements of love by never going back to hospital and never telling anyone the secrets of my newfound health.

And worse still, God forbid that I would form a little group of healthy people and condemn and avoid all the people still sick in hospital.

I felt obligated to put whatever new knowledge and experience I had of the Holy Spirit at the service of my local church and local community. These were my views and also the views of the Full Gospel Fellowship.

And those views were certainly not contradicted but rather totally affirmed by the experiences of conversions, miracles and healings I saw with my own eyes during those early Full Gospel Days.

Through those early Charismatic and Full Gospel conventions and meetings I came into a loving relationship with the God of the Catholics, the God of the Protestants, the God of the Pentecostals, the God of the Baptists, the God of the Presbyterians and all other Christian denominations.

I was meeting them and hearing their stories and I delighted in it. I was enjoying the full benefits of Psalm 133, How good and pleasant it is when God's people live together in unity!

True freedom in Christ is being able to love one another without insisting the other party jump ship and become the same as me. We need to recognise and accept one another long before we can ever be reconciled to one another. If we are judging each other from narrow minded prejudiced positions it's very hard to achieve true reconciliation.

Many people think we have to be changed before we can be reconciled. That's not true. Jesus gave us all the ministry of reconciliation and he himself had a very diverse bunch of disciples that would never have stayed together had it not been for them making Jesus the centre.

Jesus said, If I be lifted up I will draw all men onto me. That loving acceptance of one another was always a shining gem in the Full Gospel Businessmen in Ireland.

Of course there can be a difficulty with sending people back into the system. The local parish priest who maybe has little or no experience of the gifts and power of the Holy Spirit can be difficult to deal with because of his fear and insecurity. This can take a long time and a lot of patience.

Not everybody was willing or able to do this. I understand this. I won't condemn anyone for leaving or staying away from the Catholic Church.

In John 21 after Peter is reinstated by Jesus, Peter turned and saw that John was following them. When Peter saw John, he asked, Lord, what about him?

Jesus answered, If I want him to remain alive until I return, what is that to you? You must follow me.

Basically Jesus was telling Peter to follow Him and mind his own business. I think we would all benefit from this approach. Everyone will have to give a personal account of whether they were obedient to Jesus' instructions or not. It's not my job to judge or condemn fellow believers.

The Full Gospel position of remaining in your own church and releasing the blessing of the Holy Spirit was not easy. I personally haven't found it trouble-free but at least I've been able to keep an open door for the Holy Spirit in my home for over forty years.

I didn't leave my community, my family and my people and become a strange thing. I remained George McAuliffe the schoolteacher, an ordinary Catholic enjoying the New Pentecost Pope John XXIII so earnestly prayed for.

The Full Gospel Businessmen's Fellowship International was a vehicle that provided an opportunity for all sorts of people to be involved in the work of the Holy Spirit. There was novelty and variety and vitality with it. It was breaking new ground, opening new doors and creating new relationships.

At our first annual convention in 1984 we had eight hundred people for the sit down meal. When Nicky Cruz came we'd nearly a thousand people at the meeting. In the early days of our home meetings people were bussed to us each Thursday night.

Over the years all of this just petered out. Maybe it

has morphed into something else I don't entirely recognise. In Ireland unfortunately the Sectarian spirit is still strong. The enemy keeps creeping back in, quarantining and separating people. Divide and conquer is still the order of the day for Satan.

Sometimes it was a case of Catholics who left the Catholic Church becoming impatient with Catholics who remained within it. They wanted them to leave their church and community of their youth and join their wee group, which in many cases would split within a few years.

When we began our meetings very few people were speaking in tongues, prophesying or praying for the sick. Now these things are happening all over Ireland, small bright fires all over the place.

God knows what He is doing and He's always doing a new thing. God is long in preparation. We have played our part. We have been obedient to the heavenly vision of keeping the fire going in our home for over forty years in season and out of season.

Nowadays there are no more *Full Gospel Business Men's* monthly meetings in our county. I still go to the annual meetings to see my remaining friends. Sometimes I think we're like old soldiers from a long forgotten war. Our numbers are diminishing year upon year.

All things have a time and a season. God is always

doing a new thing. I love that verse in Isaiah 43 when God says,

> See, I am doing a new thing! Now it
> springs up; do you not perceive it? I
> am making a way in the wilderness
> and streams in the wasteland.

I thank God for the Full Gospel Businessmen in Ireland. I thank God for those brothers who sacrificed their time and money to bring us the good news of Jesus Christ and His Holy Spirit.

The Full Gospel Businessmen's Fellowship International has been an open hearted vehicle from God that allowed the Holy Spirit to radically impact different individuals and denominations throughout Ireland. It was a servant ministry that washed the feet of the saints.

I personally believe the Full Gospel Businessmen's Fellowship helped change Irish history for the better. For many people it was the first time physical and spiritual borders were crossed. Protestants coming South, Catholics going North. Sworn enemies embracing and praying together. Joining hands and singing,

> Bind us together Lord,
> Bind us together,
> With cords that cannot be broken,

Bind us together Lord,
Bind us together,
Bind us together in Love.

The Full Gospel Businessmen Fellowship was an instrument of reconciliation without ever intending to be. It created more genuine understanding and lasting friendships than many of the overworked reconciliation conferences. People staying in one another's homes, laughing together, eating together and opening their hearts to one another has created a lasting impact and blessing for thousands of people throughout Ireland.

When Pope John XXIII called for the first ecumenical council in the Roman Catholic Church his main heartfelt desires were for unity amongst Christians and for a 'new pentecost' in the Catholic Church.

I believe The Full Gospel Businessmen was a partial answer to the Holy Father's prayers and intentions. They were a prophetic group way ahead of their time. They certainly created space for me to minister and fellowship way beyond my limited sphere of influence in Milltown.

These were some of the things that happened in Ireland under my watch and these are things I can give honest testimony to. I know for sure that He who has begun a good work will bring it to completion. I sometimes think of 2 Timothy when St. Paul writes,

I am already being poured out like a drink
    offering, and the time for my depar-
    ture is near. I have fought the good
    fight, I have finished the race, I have
    kept the faith. Now there is in store
    for me the crown of righteousness,
    which the Lord, the righteous Judge,
    will award to me on that day and not
    only to me, but also to all who have
    longed for his appearing.

Sheila and I were so blessed to have been a small part of the new things God began to do in Ireland. I believe the best wine is yet to come. That means there'll be a need for new wineskins and new workers in the harvest.

God is alway doing a new thing. He is always working His purpose out and that purpose is always Jesus Christ.

As God says in Jeremiah, I know the plans I have for you," declares the Lord, "plans to prosper you and not to harm you, plans to give you hope and a future.

JOYFUL IN MY HOUSE OF PRAYER

RUNNING a weekly prayer meeting in our home has been effortless. There'd always be some little gem of revelation or teaching bubbling up in my heart to use as a foundation for the meeting. And out of this little trickle would flow living water that'd quench our thirsts. It has been a privilege beyond words.

When we first started meeting we were just talking about Jesus. Then we moved on to speaking to Jesus. Then we began to listen to Jesus. Then we got baptised in the Holy Spirit and started speaking in tongues and experiencing the gifts of the Holy Spirit.

Week by week and year by year the Lord led us forward and opened his treasures to us. For over forty years there has been a gentle and consistent rhythm to it all. In the beginning we might have been concerned about numbers but that left us after reading Matthew 18 and hearing Jesus say, For where two or three are gathered together in my name, there am I in the midst of them.

After I started speaking to Jesus in the meetings it was as if a straitjacket was removed from me. Like being set free from jail, set free from the claustrophobic prison of conventional prayer and ritual. I came to realise the Christian life is a continual process of revelation, transformation and release. If the Son shall set you free you shall be free indeed.

For over forty years our door has been open to the work of the Holy Spirit. I don't think I ever asked anybody apart from Vincent to ever come to our meeting. After we'd been going for five or six weeks Sheila and I had a little disagreement, which was unusual for us.

This troubled me so I went up into the local Catholic Church on Sunday afternoon to pray about it. In church I found a little scrap of writing paper to my right under the seat. Scribbled on it were the words, *I will make your house a house of prayer.* I was greatly encouraged by this.

More recently I read in Isaiah 56 where God speaks about those who do what is right and please him. He says, These I will bring to my holy mountain, and make them joyful in my house of prayer. He also says, My house will be called a house of prayer for all nations. I love that phrase, *joyful in my house of prayer.* It so aptly describes the ministry God gave Sheila and me.

Sheila and I never wrote out a vision or a mission statement for our meetings. Yet over the years so many people from so many nations have found their way to our home in Milltown. One night Brian Nicholson from Cork joined us. During worship Brian suddenly stood up and said, The Lord is pleased with the faithfulness of this little group.

I must admit I didn't pay much heed to this word apart from the fact that Brian was trying to encourage us.

With eyes tightly closed Brian held up his left hand. He said, The Lord is telling me he wants to heal somebody here with a broken bone in their left elbow. Yes, it is the left elbow and it has been broken for many years.

Lillian Healey, sitting in the corner showed some interest. I acknowledged her interest and went on with the meeting. At the end of the meeting I went over to her and said, What's this about your left elbow?

Lillian explained that fourteen years previously she'd broken her left elbow. But the doctor hadn't realised it was broken so it had set incorrectly. Periodically over the years this elbow would cause her great pain. Six months previously the pain was so bad the doctor ordered an x-ray and discovered it had been broken. The doctor suggested breaking it again and resetting it.

I said, How does this affect your arm?

She held out her left hand. There was movement in the wrist but the arm was rigid. Brian and I prayed for her. Within seconds she fell on the floor under the power of the Holy Spirit.

I said, Let's see if ye can move your elbow now.

With a big smile on her face she twisted her arm this way and that way. Total flexibility and movement had been restored in an instant.

Months later I met Lillian again. I said, You should go and get your arm x-rayed again and we can compare the two x-rays.

Lillian smiled and thrust out her left arm and rotated it with ease. She said, That's all the proof I need.

I've often pondered on Brian's prophecy that the Lord was pleased with the faithfulness of our little group. Seemed to me God had spoken and immediately confirmed his word with signs following, the sign being the healing of Lillian's elbow.

That same night Brian also prophesied on the basis of Revelation 3. He read,

> These are the words of him who is holy
> and true, who holds the key of David.
> What he opens no one can shut, and
> what he shuts no one can open. I know

your deeds. See, I have placed before
you an open door that no one can shut.
I know that you have little strength, yet
you have kept my word and have not
denied my name. I will make those
who are of the synagogue of Satan,
who claim to be Jews though they are
not, but are liars.
I will make them come and fall down at
your feet and acknowledge that I have
loved you. Since you have kept my
command to endure patiently, I will
also keep you from the hour of trial
that is going to come on the whole
world to test the inhabitants of the
earth.
I am coming soon. Hold on to what you
have, so that no one will take your
crown.

As I reflected on Brian's prophecies I was heartened
by his serious and encouraging words from God.

Over the years seasons came and went. For some it
was a time to be born. For others a time to die. I
enjoyed leading people to faith in Jesus. I was blessed to
sit with dying friends and neighbours. I'd read Paul's
words from Thessalonians 4,

Brothers and sisters, we do not want you
    to be uninformed about those who
    sleep in death, so that you do not
    grieve like the rest of mankind, who
    have no hope.
For we believe that Jesus died and rose
    again, and so we believe that God will
    bring with Jesus those who have fallen
    asleep in him.
According to the Lord's word, we tell you
    that we who are still alive, who are left
    until the coming of the Lord, will
    certainly not precede those who have
    fallen asleep.
For the Lord himself will come down
    from heaven, with a loud command,
    with the voice of the archangel and
    with the trumpet call of God, and the
    dead in Christ will rise first.
After that, we who are still alive and are
    left will be caught up together with
    them in the clouds to meet the Lord in
    the air. And so we will be with the
    Lord forever. Therefore encourage
    one another with these words.

I'm totally convinced of an after life. I wholeheart-
edly agree with Paul who in I Corinthians 15 says,

If only for this life we have hope in Christ,
   we are of all people most to be pitied.
   But Christ has indeed been raised
   from the dead, the first fruits of those
   who have fallen asleep.
For since death came through a man, the
   resurrection of the dead comes also
   through a man. For as in Adam all die,
   so in Christ all will be made alive.

One summer just before school reopened I was struck down with gallbladder trouble. The doctor arranged for my gallbladder to be removed by keyhole surgery but halfway through the operation they had to resort to the conventional method of opening me up and stitching me up.

I wakened up, wound up and wired up, in the intensive care unit. In the background I could hear a man talking non-stop to a nurse. Turned out this was Dennis Conway a famous local character and pub owner who'd just had a heart attack. He just lived a few hundred yards from the hospital.

Dennis was very funny and a great storyteller. He also complained about everything and anything in very colourful language. He mentioned his son Francie who played music with The Furey Brothers. He talked about how they all went on a boat in Holland for Francie's wedding. His voice and stories helped to distract my attention and ease my pain.

I was then moved to a two-bedded ward. I was experiencing excruciating back pain they attributed to the surgery. But a couple of days later when they were fixing my bedclothes I was accidentally touched on my back and the ache exploded. This alerted the doctor to the fact my back pain had nothing to do with the operation. This was the only time in my life I suffered from sciatica.

Next day Dennis was put in the bed beside me. He complained about this. He complained about that. Sometimes it wasn't funny. That night my sciatica pain kept me awake.

As I lay in the darkness I thought, If I was to die tonight I know where I'd go. But if that poor complainer in the next bed was to die what would happen to him? Then perhaps he'd really have something to complain about.

I decided I'd not let the next morning pass without sharing my testimony of Jesus with Dennis.

Immediately upon wakening Dennis opened a little door for me to speak to him.

He said, George I've been dreaming about death and dying all-night long.

I said, Dennis, if you had died during the night where do you think you'd be now?

Ahh, I don't know, he said. Sure nobody knows

what happens at all when you die. Nobody has ever come back to tell us.

I started speaking about Jesus and sharing my story and to my surprise Dennis was like a thirsty cat being given fresh milk. He lapped it up and meowed for more. All day long he kept asking me questions. After supper I said, Dennis I think I should pray with you now so you'll be filled with the Holy Spirit.

He came over to my bed for I was still attached to a drip. I then prayed with him to be filled with the Holy Spirit and to have peace and so on. Shortly afterwards he went to sleep. Next morning his first words to me were, George in all my life I've never felt so much joy as I have this morning.

When the doctor did his rounds Dennis insisted on staying in hospital for another day to hear more about Jesus. Previously he complained about everything and wanted to get out as quickly as possible. Later that day as he was being taken for a cardiograph I overheard him talking to a nurse.

He said, I've never in all my life heard anything like I've heard from that man in the bed next to me.

Next day Dennis went home. Afterwards one by one the nurses came and talked with me. They wanted to know what I'd said that had excited Dennis the Complainer so much. A month later I was convalescing at home when news came that Dennis had dropped dead.

I spoke with his wife at the funeral. She said Dennis was a changed man after he came home from hospital. He immediately went and bought a Bible and started reading it. He stopped swearing and started praying.

Denis was one of the funniest men I ever met. Now I know there'll be humour in heaven.

OUR BAGS ARE PACKED

IN MARCH 2006 our children clubbed together and gave Sheila and me the gift of holiday in Spain. We were due to travel on Sunday the 5th March.

On Thursday 2nd March I picked up Sheila from Killarney bus station. She was coming from Cork where she'd been babysitting our grandson for a couple of days. We also collected our holiday tickets from Killorglin.

Back home Sheila wanted to go for a walk but I was expecting two young people for a math's lesson and needed some rest before their arrival. Sheila put a little pressure on me to go for a walk with her. This was unusual for her.

I said, Darling I really need to rest.

While she was gone for some reason I began to think how things might be if Sheila were dead. I pondered life without Sheila. I knew I'd be gutted, feeling deprived and heartbroken. I imagined saying to myself, Oh what would I not give if Sheila were to walk through this door again to be with me.

Then I thought, In a few minutes time Sheila really will walk in that door to be with me. So I will give her the kind of welcome I'd give her if she really had come back from the dead. So when she opened the back door I jumped up and embraced her with great warmth as if she were coming from a far country.

On our journey to Cork the previous Tuesday we had discussed the naturalness of Jesus after he'd risen from the dead. He'd asked for fish to eat. Imagine someone raised from the dead walking around looking for a piece of fish. I wondered where that Scripture came in the gospel. Sheila started looking through her New Testament.

She said, Seoirse, I have found the words you mentioned. She started reading from Luke 24. She read the whole chapter. I especially remember verses 45-49,

> Then he opened their minds so they could
> understand the Scriptures. He told
> them, This is what is written: The
> Messiah will suffer and rise from the
> dead on the third day, and repentance
> for the forgiveness of sins will be
> preached in his name to all

nations, beginning at Jerusalem. You are witnesses of these things. I am going to send you what my Father has promised; but stay in the city until you have been clothed with power from on high.

Although Jesus had been with his disciples for three and a half years he still needed to open their minds so they could understand the scriptures about him. Opening our minds was the very thing Jesus had done for Sheila and me over the many years at our weekly prayer meetings. He had opened our minds to understand his Bible and the gifts and working of His Holy Spirit.

We often prayed he'd do the same for millions of ordinary Catholics just like us all over the world. Jesus also promised to send the Holy Spirit who would cover His people with heavenly power. This was the baptism of the Holy Spirit we'd experienced and the power we'd experienced and seen especially in the early days of Full Gospel Businessmen in Kerry.

In our weekly prayer meeting on 2nd March 2006, Sheila shared a long scripture about the elders in heaven bowing down and praising the Lord. I remember her hand waving with excitement as she read from Revelation 4;

After this I looked, and there before me was a door standing open in heaven. And the voice I had first heard speaking to me like a trumpet said, Come up here, and I will show you what must take place after this. At once I was in the Spirit, and there before me was a throne in heaven with someone sitting on it. And the one who sat there had the appearance of jasper and ruby. A rainbow that shone like an emerald encircled the throne.

Surrounding the throne were twenty-four other thrones, and seated on them were twenty-four elders. They were dressed in white and had crowns of gold on their heads. From the throne came flashes of lightning, rumblings and peals of thunder. In front of the throne, seven lamps were blazing. These are the seven spirits of God. Also in front of the throne there was what looked like a sea of glass, clear as cryst

In the centre around the throne, were four living creatures, and they were

covered with eyes, in front and in
back. The first living creature was like
a lion, the second was like an ox, the
third had a face like a man, the fourth
was like a flying eagle.

Each of the four living creatures had six
wings and was covered with eyes all
around, even under its wings. Day and
night they never stop saying: Holy,
holy, holy is the Lord God Almighty,
who was, and is, and is to come.

Whenever the living creatures give glory,
honour and thanks to him who sits on
the throne and who lives forever and
ever, the twenty-four elders fall down
before him who sits on the throne and
worship him who lives forever and
ever.

They lay their crowns before the throne
and say: You are worthy, our Lord and
God, to receive glory and honour and
power, for you created all things, and
by your will they were created and
have their being.

That night, Sheila went to bed while I finished watching a television program. We always shared a little routine with the daily crossword. Sheila would do it first and I'd then try to finish it before the end of the day.

When I went into our bedroom Sheila was sound asleep, the crossword almost complete. I finished all but for one clue.

Next morning over breakfast we had another look at the crossword. I still couldn't figure out the clue but suddenly Sheila got it.

She said, Crown! Why didn't I think of it sooner?

The answer to the clue was the word *crown*.

I said, Fair dues Sheila. You're as good as ever!

Sheila said, Seoirse, remember I mentioned crowns in my reading last night.

I said, You did indeed Darling. You also left a note for me about crowns recently.

Six weeks previously Sheila had been at a Lydia Fellowship conference and had felt very peaceful and blessed afterwards. Someone had spoken on scriptures about the crowns available to believers.

Later Sheila left a note for me saying, God is our refuge and strength, an ever-present help in trouble. Further down the page she had written,

> Now there is in store for me the crown of
> righteousness, which the Lord, the

righteous Judge, will award to me on
that day and not only to me, but also to
all who have longed for his appearing. [1]

We then discussed the issue of Christian crowns for
a few minutes. We mentioned the five heavenly crowns
mentioned in the New Testament that will be awarded
to faithful believers, the imperishable crown, the crown
of rejoicing, the crown of righteousness, the crown of
glory, and the crown of life.

Sheila then read St. Paul's words from the end of 1
Corinthians 9,

To the weak I became weak, to win the
weak. I have become all things to all
people so that by all possible means I
might save some. I do all this for the
sake of the gospel, that I may share in
its blessings.
Do you not know that in a race all the
runners run, but only one gets the
prize? Run in such a way as to get the
prize.
Everyone who competes in the games
goes into strict training. They do it for
a crown that will not last but we do it
for a crown that will last forever.
Therefore I do not run like someone

running aimlessly; I do not fight like a
boxer beating the air. No, I strike a
blow to my body and make it my slave
so that after I have preached to others,
I myself will not be disqualified for the
prize.

Sheila looked at me and said, Seoirse, we must make
sure we finish our race well and receive our crowns
from Jesus!

Outside it was a beautiful March morning, cold and
dry, the gorse and daffodils glowing in the sun. Sheila
was a volunteer with the Samaritans. She had a shift
with them from 11am to 2pm that day.

She touched her cheek and said, I think I have a
touch of neuralgia this morning.

Both of us took no further notice of that.

We were excited about our upcoming holiday. I
rushed off to Killorglin to fetch our new passports from
the police station. When I was collecting the passports
the police telephone rang.

The guard said, Mr McAuliffe it's for you. He
handed me the phone.

It was Sheila asking me to collect travel insurance
from a nearby office.

Back home Sheila was pleased that everything was
now ready. We looked at our two new suitcases
waiting patiently in our hallway.

Sheila said my friend Gabriel had rang and she'd arranged for him and me to play a round of golf. Shortly afterwards Gabriel drove into our yard and I put my clubs into his boot and climbed into his car.

Just as we were about to take off Sheila ran laughing from the house clutching a bottle of water.

I said, Thank you my love! You're always kind and thinking of others.

Sheila said, Sure it's only a bottle of water. Remember to keep hydrated.

Just then Lillian Healy who was travelling to Tralee with Sheila was dropped off in the yard.

Sheila hugged Lillian and turned back to me smiling, the sunlight shining on her hair.

She said, It won't be long now, Seoirse!

We parted.

A strange incident occurred on the golf course. For a few minutes it seemed as if my body was on the golf course but my spirit was somewhere else. In the middle of the twelfth fairway, for no particular reason, I found myself saying very deliberately and very loudly, Where I live there was once five women called Sheila. There was Sheila O'Connor, Sheila Horgan, Sheila Keller, Sheila Conway, and Sheila McAuliffe, and the only one alive today is my Sheila.

Afterwards, I came home to an empty house. Sheila had taken our car.

I checked my suitcase one more time to make sure

everything was ready. Then I decided I'd walk up to the barbers for a holiday haircut.

The phone rang.

A voice said, George McAuliffe?

Yes.

Married to Sheila McAuliffe?

Yes.

I wondered where this conversation was going?

He said, I'm calling from Samaritans to inform you that Sheila has got a weakness.

Is she all right?

He said Yes, she's okay. She's gone to hospital.

I said, Thank you for telling me.

He put the phone down.

I pondered for a while. I thought there might be more to it then he was admitting to.

I rang back.

He answered.

I said, Was Sheila conscious when she was taken to hospital?

He said, No she wasn't. She went in an ambulance.

He explained what happened. Dennis O'Brien a Full Gospel man, was waiting outside Sheila's cubicle to replace her on the telephone. As Dennis watched, Sheila finished her call, hung up the phone and immediately lost consciousness. Dennis's wife had suffered a stroke, so he knew exactly what was happening. He called an ambulance and started praying. This occurred around 2pm.

This was an entirely different picture. I became very troubled by the thought of Sheila hospitalised in an unconscious state.

I rang our daughter Emer who was working in Tralee.

I said, Emer, Mammy's in hospital in Tralee. Perhaps you should go to see what's happening. I've no car but I'll get over as soon as I can.

I ran up to McCarthy's, our next-door neighbours. There was no one at home. I walked back towards our house out of breath. Gerald McCarthy was driving home when he saw me leaving his house. He followed me and loaned me his car.

At the hospital I was put into a side room. Emer entered.

I asked, How are things Love?

She said, Not good Da.

I said, Will she be alright?

She said, I don't think things are good.

After a while a consultant spoke to Emer and me.

He said, What way do you want me to tell this?

I said, Please tell it exactly as it is.

He said, Well, Mr McAuliffe your wife is going to die within a couple of hours or at most a day. Do you want me to do anything?

I said, No! Let nature take its course. I don't believe in tinkering around the edges of an event.

Emer said, Da, Muireann is in London. Maybe we can do something until she arrives.

I said, Okay Love!

They decided to leave Sheila on the ventilator.

I was taken into intensive care. Sheila looked exactly the same as she always did. Beautiful to my eyes! I didn't know how to react. I just had to bide my time and wait for things to run their course.

I rang the children with the news that something big was happening and they needed to be here immediately.

Aoife said, But Daddy, won't Mammy be alright?

It broke my heart to say, No Darling, the doctor says she won't. You have to come as soon as possible.

One by one our children gathered. Muireann was the last to arrive around 9pm. We were a family again for one last time, Muireann, Emer, Joseph, Deirdre, Aoife, John, Sheila and myself. A family huddled together in sorrow and love.

Someone said, Mammy we love you more than we can say but you are now free to go. And they all took up this chorus, each voice echoing the sentiments of the whole family.

Mummy we love you but you're free to move on.

Go Darling, now.

We will be all right Mammy.

Thanks for everything Mammy.

You're the best Mammy is the whole world.

A verse from Psalms kept floating in my mind, *Precious in the eyes of the Lord is the death of his loved ones.*

After a while the children went to a room next door, and I was left alone with Sheila. I held her hand. I now knew Sheila had completed the last part of her crossword upon this earth and was now receiving her crown of righteousness from Jesus. I prayed with her and told her I loved her.

The children came back in and started speaking more love to their Mammy, reassuring her we'd all be all right, saying they'd look after Daddy.

I knew Sheila was probably no longer in her body but was likely floating above the room watching us with love as we gazed upon her dying body. I knew the one we all loved so much was giving up her spirit and returning to the One who loved her most of all. The silver cord was finally being broken.

Then after another outburst of telling her we loved her Sheila straightened up on her elbow a couple of times, breathed deeply and was gone. She looked the picture of peace. *Precious in the eyes of the Lord is the death of His saints.*

Sheila died at 12.25am on Saturday 5th March 2006 just over ten hours after she lost consciousness.

The windscreens of our cars were frozen when we left the hospital an hour later. One of the children fetched hot water and I remembered how earlier it was decided the children would go home and I would stay in the bedroom next door to Sheila.

I breathed into my cold hands and looked far off into the starry frosty night. I thought, Typical of Sheila. She even spared me the trouble of having to stay overnight in hospital.

Sheila died as she lived, a handmaiden of the Lord. Washing the feet of the saints. There were no unfinished issues with Sheila. She had reared her children and though she hadn't seen them all married or held all their lovely babies she had done her bit. Her bags were packed and she was ready to go.

The day Sheila died my brother back on the home farm in Brosna was looking through a bundle of old paperwork searching for cards to do with his cattle when he found a little cutting of David's obituary. He put it in his wallet intending to give it to us. He then came into town only to be told Sheila was dying in the local hospital.

A little tender linking – David's death – Sheila's death – both joyfully regretted.

I love these little signs of God's fingerprints on our lives. His little tender tokens of love.

THREE TIMES A LADY

AROUND CHRISTMAS TIME, the year before Sheila died, I was asked to give a reflection during Sunday Mass on the importance of family. Sheila was to do an accompanying reading. There was a huge crowd. Standing room only.

Before Mass Sheila said, Seoirse do you have the notes for your reflection?

I remembered putting them into my jacket pocket. I felt for them. Paper rustled.

I do, I said.

Within fifteen minutes of my talk I pulled them out and discovered instead of my reflection notes I'd brought an article by a priest about there being far too much noise in our lives.

Sheila said, Is everything all right Seoirse?

I said, Unfortunately not Darling I've brought the wrong notes.

Where are they?

Perhaps on the kitchen table?

Sheila slipped out of the pew. Our car was blocked in due to the big crowd. She persuaded someone to drive her down to our house. She couldn't find the notes. She came back up again and searched our car. Still no notes. She slipped back in beside me just before her reading and my talk.

She said, I'm so sorry Seoirse. I couldn't find your notes. What will you do?

I said, I'll do what I can.

I stood in the pulpit and gazed over the crowded church. I said, You might have noticed during the last few minutes Sheila my wife has been in and out of the church. The reason for that was I thought I had my reflection notes in my pocket when in fact I had a different piece of paper altogether.

When Sheila realised my dilemma she immediately jumped to my defence. Sheila actually spent a lot of time getting me and our children out of difficult situations.

She was like one of the women in the Bible who boldly brought their children before Jesus. Sheila was a great demonstration of what family life is all about. I think of Ecclesiastes 4,

Two are better than one because they
have a good return for their labour: If
either of them falls down, one can help
the other up. But pity anyone who falls
and has no one to help them up. Also,
if two lie down together, they will keep
warm. But how can one keep warm
alone? Though one may be overpow-
ered, two can defend themselves. A
cord of three strands is not quickly
broken.

That's how I honoured Sheila and reflected on family; a unit of love and consideration, supporting and encouraging one another. Laying down their lives for one another. Carrying one another's burdens. Just like Sheila was so willing to help carry my burden.

Family is a beautiful thing. In the end I was glad I'd lost my notes for this gave me an opportunity to praise Sheila before the whole community.

Later the priest said, By God I wouldn't like to go up there without my sheet of paper when I'm doing a homily.

I'm so grateful for the gift that Sheila was in my life. She truly was a blessing from God. Proverbs 18:22 says, The man who finds a wife finds a treasure, and he receives favour from the Lord. Proverbs 19:14 says, Fathers can give their sons an inheritance of houses and wealth, but only the Lord can give an understanding wife.

In Corinthians 13 Paul talks about love. I feel I could substitute the name Sheila for the word love and it would still make sense to me. Paul said,

> Love is patient, love is kind. It does not
> envy, it does not boast, it is not proud.
> It does not dishonour others, it is not
> self-seeking, it is not easily angered, it
> keeps no record of wrongs. Love does
> not delight in evil but rejoices with the
> truth. It always protects, always trusts,
> always hopes, always perseveres. Love
> never fails.

Sheila was patient and kind. She bore no wrong. She wasn't opinionated. She blessed and loved all sorts of people. She was gentle. She had courage. At her funeral many people said she was a real lady.

My reply was, If she was a lady outside of the house she was infinitely more of a lady inside the house.

When Sheila would give her testimony she'd say that when I decided to go for broke and abandon the old reliable certainties and seek the Lord and the gifts of the Holy Spirit she felt compelled to ensure that at least one of us kept our feet on the ground. She became a foil to my enthusiasm.

But then one day while she was washing the dishes the revelation came to her about praise and worship as well. Afterwards she joined with me in the full-hearted exuberance and abandonment of trusting and praising God full time.

We often prayed and read and discussed the Bible together. We went to Mass together. We attended weddings, wakes, funerals, baptisms, first communions, confirmations and all other important events in the parish and community together.

We loved our Thursday night meetings where we met and functioned with other Holy Spirit filled believers. Faithful ones who'd been our true friends for donkey's years. Fellowship with believers from all denominations was important to us.

Often we'd attend other churches and meetings as well as Charismatic and Full Gospel conventions. We gave a few years to the marriage encounter program and worked with many groups through that.

Sheila was patient with the children. When I'd come home from school she'd regularly be sitting with a child in her arms reading a story or singing a song. Sheila was a beautiful singer and a lovely violinist. She would always give a party piece on her fiddle and then laugh happily at her performance.

I remember Sheila like this; if I went into a crowded room of people looking for her I could almost see a glow in the part of the room where she was and I'd be attracted to that glow.

Sheila marched to a different drum. One Sunday our family were supporting one of our sons who playing football for the county team. At one stage a player from the opposing team scored what was an excellent point. The other crowd went wild with cheering. Sheila started clapping and cheering along with them.

We were outraged. One of the children said, Mammy why on earth are you cheering him?

Sheila said, Because Darling, he's some mother's son and she'll be proud of him and so am I.

When we were out and about in our car Sheila would do her share of driving. If she'd start going a little too fast I'd say, Sheila my pet, you are hurtling.

A few minutes later I might say, Sheila you're still hurtling.

Sheila would say, Seoirse, how come the car only hurtles when I'm driving?

Occasionally I'd say, Sheila, if anything happens to you I'll be all right.

I wanted to assure her I'd survive until we met again in Heaven. Reassure her I wouldn't go on the drink or fall into despair. A couple of years before she died I'd occasionally get this vague picture of myself in a life after Sheila.

The picture was of myself standing unapologetically

and unashamedly in the middle of a group of people at our prayer meeting praising the Lord with more gusto than ever.

So from the very first prayer meeting after her death until now I have been faithful to that heavenly vision. Whenever I remember that vision I am strengthened and grateful to God who showed me things to come.

Sheila walked into my life in 1965 and walked out of it again just over forty years later. Sheila came into my ordinary life and changed it forever for the better. Then just over forty years later she walked out of our new life together and now awaits me in heaven, when my time has come, when my story's told.

Some people have asked me do I pray to Sheila. Of course I don't pray to Sheila. I only pray to the Father in Jesus' name. This is what Jesus told us to do. For a lifetime I have prayed with Sheila. I have never prayed to her. More than likely she is praying for me.

Sheila's sudden death at age sixty-three shocked the whole community. When the undertaker arrived, I assumed we'd use the funeral parlour but the children wanted to wake their mammy at home. Sheila's death was a sharp knife twisting in our hearts. I've never felt so much pain.

On Sunday afternoon when Sheila's remains were moved to the funeral parlour there was a mile long queue and a traffic jam on the road. People said it was the biggest funeral ever in our area. In the evening we took her to the church. The children and myself had each written a farewell letter to her. Later I went up to the church opened the coffin and put in our letters. I also put in something else.

Early next morning I fetched a black plastic bag from the shed and went up to the graveyard. Sheila died in springtime when the local crows were preparing their nests. On her funeral morning I walked to her grave before Mass.

There was a choir of crows in the graveyard trees cawing at the top of their lungs reminding me that although Sheila was dead not everything was dead. Spring had returned like a child that knows poetry but my heart would be in the grave with Sheila for many lonely days to come.

I like crows. They have extraordinary vision. They are intelligent. There is no pretence with crows. Like myself they make a joyful noise unto the Lord. To me they represent great energy, the hustle and bustle of life. I thought of Jesus speaking;

> I say to you, do not be worried about your
>   life, as to what you will eat or what
>   you will drink; nor for your body, as to
>   what you will put on. Is not life more
>   than food, and the body more than
>   clothing?

Look at the birds of the air, that they do
   not sow, nor reap nor gather into
   barns, and yet your heavenly Father
   feeds them. Are you not worth much
   more than they? And who of you by
   being worried can add a single hour to
   his life?

I became very calm and peaceful. I jumped into the
newly opened grave and raised my hands. Sheila often
said, Seoirse, your special song is, *I Will Enter His Gates*.
So I stood in the grave and I sang,

   I will enter His gates
   With thanksgiving in my heart
   I will enter His courts with praise
   I will say this is the day that the Lord
      has made
   I will rejoice for He has made me glad.
   He has made me glad; He has made me
      glad,
   I will rejoice for he has made me glad
   He has made me glad; He has made me
      glad,
   I will rejoice for he has made me glad

It felt like I'd brought our prayer meeting from our
home into the very grave itself. I knelt on the black bag

and prayed and offered God a sacrifice of praise. I could still hear the crows in the background. I sang another old favourite,

> There is never a reason strong enough
> For not praising the Lord.
> Whenever the going's getting tough
> You've got to keep praising the Lord.
>
> Praise him, you know that you should
> Everything's working together for good
> Praise him, you can never afford
> To ever stop praising the Lord.

Sheila's funeral Mass was packed with people from all over Ireland from all denominations and traditions. The service was lovely, the singing wonderful. The priest called Sheila the quintessential lady. It was an appropriate description.

As we followed her coffin up to the graveyard I remembered Sheila and me hand in hand following David's little white coffin thirty-three years earlier.

Although Sheila was no longer holding my hand, our lovely children were clustered around me, stalwarts, standing up and standing by me. I thought of Psalm 127 that says happy is the man who has his quiver full of children for he will not be put to shame when he meets with his enemies in the gate. I had met with death in the gate and my children stood with me in my hour of need.

At the grave I spoke to honour Sheila. I talked about the Friday night when she died. I said, That wasn't when Sheila met her Lord for the first time. She met her Lord and Saviour many years earlier when she gave her life to Jesus Christ.

On Friday night when she died she didn't meet with a stranger but with someone whom she had loved and worshipped and praised for nearly forty years.

I mentioned it was customary for Sheila and me, when we passed the funeral home, to remind ourselves that one day one of us would be looking at the remains of the other. At these times we'd pray for power and strength and peace for the one who would remain. We used the presence of the funeral home to remind us of our privilege and duty towards one another.

Not long before Sheila died I myself had a cancer scare. Some of our children were speaking to us concerning the situation.

Someone said, Dad you know we could be speaking about death here.

I said, I know but I'm ready for whatever comes my way. I'm like Pope John XXIII who said on his deathbed, My bag is packed and I'm ready to go.

Sheila and I went to to see the cancer specialist. The doctor said there'd be surgery, chemotherapy and radiotherapy. Sheila was upset.

I had an MRI scan. While in that machine I'd a strong sense that I was in communication with someone beyond whom it was neither necessary nor possible to go, my Heavenly Father. When all the scans and tests were completed they couldn't find a single trace of cancer.

The registrar said, Someone will get a rap on the knuckles for this.

Sheila and I came home rejoicing with my small suitcase unopened. Recently I had an operation for a melanoma on my nose. These things remind us of our own mortality. Every generation everybody dies.

I sometimes think of the aged Éamon de Valera who said, The curiosity of the next life is getting the better of me.

Normally I'm not a great dreamer but a couple of years after Sheila's death I had two similar dreams close together. In both dreams Sheila and I were playing hide and seek and having great fun.

When the children were young I'd sometimes turn off the lights and we'd all play hide and seek in our living room. We always enjoyed the sniggers, squeals and gusts of laughter.

In one dream I was back in my home place in Brosna. At one point I slipped into a darkened cowshed to hide from Sheila. I leaned back against a wall and stayed as quiet as possible. Down at my foot a little calf started to move. I hoped it would stop otherwise it might betray my position.

Just then Sheila peeked around the shed door and was momentarily blinded by the darkness. Then she spied me and immediately a beautiful smile lit up her lovely face.

When this happened a pleasant bolt of warmth, peace and healing, physically hit me. I woke up at this point with a wonderful sensation of being blessed and healed and loved and accepted.

Like in Isaiah 61, I felt so comforted. I'd been given a crown of beauty instead of ashes, oil instead of mourning and a garment of praise instead of a spirit of despair.

That sweet feeling stayed with me for three days and healed me.

NOTES

4. SOMETHING BEAUTIFUL FOR GOD

1. Galatians 2:20

5. A LITTLE CHILD SHALL LEAD THEM

1. Matthew 16:25

7. THE CATHOLIC CHARISMATIC MOVEMENT.

1. John 3:8

13. OUR BAGS ARE PACKED

1. 2 Timothy 4:8

Printed in Great Britain
by Amazon